Universal Worklist with SAP NetWe

Darren Hague

MW01099176

Contents

Contents

Foreword

In April 2006, SAP ERP was introduced into Vodafone's head office operations to replace a number of legacy systems that were previously utilized throughout the business. (Vodafone Group's global headquarters are in the United Kingdom, and there are also significant operations in Germany together with a number of smaller operations in other parts of the world.) The initial launch introduced the Finance, HCM, SRM, and Business Intelligence modules, all integrated via the SAP NetWeaver Portal, which was accessed via Single Sign-on from Vodafone's intranet.

The Universal Worklist (UWL) is a key component of Vodafone's SAP installation, as it is the UWL that combines the various workflow requests from the different SAP modules into a single location for the users to access. In addition, the UWL manages the process for when people are on vacation and require other staff members to undertake their tasks while they are away from the office.

As a mobile telecommunications company and with a significant part of the user base traveling, Vodafone intro-duced the ability for managers to approve shopping carts on their BlackBerry® handheld devices from day one. Managers receive an email informing them that they have received a shopping cart for approval and then click a link to open the SAP NetWeaver Portal on their BlackBerry. They can then review the details of the shopping cart on their BlackBerry and decide whether to approve or reject the cart.

This book provides an in-depth guide to the Universal Worklist and its related technologies, including Black-Berry-based approval. It will help you get the most out of your company's investment in SAP, not to mention its investment in mobile telecommunications.

Campbell Smith
Finance Executive
Vodafone Group Services Limited

1 Introduction

This book covers the Universal Worklist (UWL) feature of the SAP NetWeaver Portal, Release 7.0 (formerly known as SAP NetWeaver 2004s). Most of what is written here is also applicable to the SAP NetWeaver Portal 2004 (EP6). In particular, the XML configurations are virtually identical; the major differences between the two versions lie in the user interface, some performance tuning options, and the new wizard-based configuration options available in SAP NetWeaver Portal 7.0.

References to the documentation on the SAP Help Portal (*http://help.sap.com*) are listed in **bold** type, with the navigation path separated by bullet points (•). For your convenience, the direct browser links for all of the referenced sections are listed in Appendix B.

What Is Workflow?

Workflow, business task management, and business process modeling are all aspects of implementing business processes that involve more than one person or system. Processes that involve a single person using a single system are done using programs or applications. For example, you may have a process for producing a project plan, but if this process only includes you and a copy of Microsoft Project, then this is not a workflow or Business Process in the accepted sense. However, if you produce a copy of the project plan that is then approved by your manager, and the tasks in that plan are monitored and updated by team members as the project progresses, then you have a workflow situation.

SAP Business Workflow allows business processes to be designed and run from within a single SAP instance, presenting individual users with their tasks using the SAP Inbox via a SAP GUI. Although these workflows can talk to other systems, they are mostly used for processes within a SAP ERP, SAP CRM, or SAP SRM instance, and

users have to log in to each instance to see the tasks for that business function.

What Is Universal Worklist?

SAP has had a Business Workflow engine for some time, and there is an excellent book on the subject: *Practical Workflow for SAP* (SAP PRESS, 2002). More recently, SAP NetWeaver has evolved to allow business processes across several systems using SAP NetWeaver Process Integration and Guided Procedures.

To meet the challenge of working with processes that run across multiple systems and to avoid the situation of users having to log in to several systems to see their work items, SAP developed the user interface of choice for SAP NetWeaver-based business process management, the Universal Worklist (UWL).

The UWL is a portal-based technology that brings all of a user's work items from a number of systems into a central point of access. Figure 1.1 shows an example of this. Users can access the details of work items by clicking on buttons or links shown in the list. In each case, UWL takes care of back end server processing, launching a dedicated portal user interface, or launching the back end application itself to process the work item.

The real business aim behind all of this, and much of what follows in this book, is to make it really easy for your users to make their decisions in a portal environment:

▶ **Usability**

You can feed the results back into the SAP Business Workflow (or other systems) without having to face the complexity of a SAP GUI transaction screen.

▶ **Substitution**

Another useful feature of the UWL is that users can define substitutes for when they are ill or on vacation. For the period of time defined by a user (assuming the recipient agrees and has the right authorizations), a

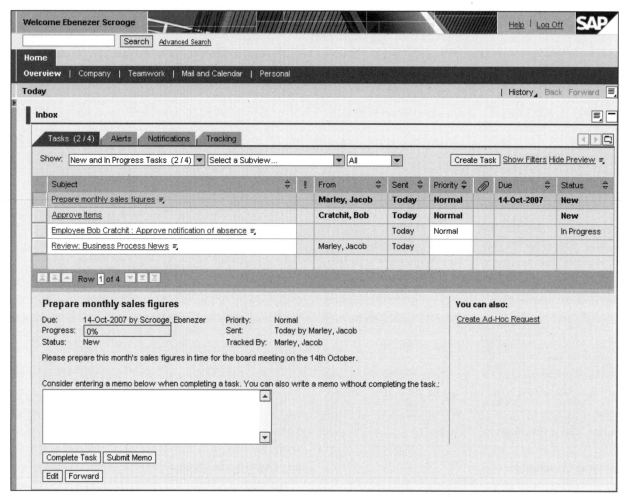

Figure 1.1 UWL Showing Items from Several Workflow Systems

substitute will receive all of a user's work items and will be able to process them, as long as the workflow system in each case supports the notion of substitution. SAP's workflow systems do support substitution, of course.

▶ **Composite applications**

Composite applications are applications or processes that appear to the user as a single, unified front end but, in fact, run on different back end systems according to the stage of the process (for example, a New Starter process might involve buying a laptop, creating an email account, and setting up systems access — each of these actions might be processed on a different system but by the same administrative user). By providing a single front end to the tasks in a composite application, the UWL enables composite applications in SAP NetWeaver.

▶ **Enterprise Service-Oriented Architecture**

SAP's vision for an Enterprise Service-Oriented Architecture (Enterprise SOA) relies on business-relevant functions and processes being exposed as Web Services so that new, higher-level processes and applications can be orchestrated and composed rather than having to be coded from scratch. SAP NetWeaver provides the platform for Enterprise SOA, and UWL can use this platform to help make composite applications and guided procedure-based processes easy to build and use.

What You Will Learn

This book is aimed at portal consultants, workflow consultants, and business process experts who are interested in making the human-facing parts of business processes more accessible.

8

You will learn the basics of setting up and working with the UWL (see **Chapter 2**) before going on to more advanced topics governing how the UWL looks and feels, and how to customize the behavior of various actions (see **Chapter 3**). After you have UWL working with a SAP Business Workflow system, you will see how to connect to other SAP and non-SAP Business Workflow systems and how to use guided procedures to implement simple custom processes using a service-oriented architecture (see **Chapter 4**). In **Chapter 5**, you'll get a look behind the scenes to see how UWL works in detail, which will help you with debugging and performance tuning. In **Chapter 6**, you'll find out about some other technologies for exposing business processes to users, including how to use a BlackBerry handheld device for processing certain kinds of work item on the move.

There are plenty of screenshots throughout the book, so you will be able to get a good overview of a configuration or programming task just by skimming through and looking at the pictures before you check out the text for a more detailed explanation. To help you further, you can find all of the source code and the documentation links and resources from the book at the SAP PRESS website, where you will also be able to find out about new and updated material.

A Note on the Examples

This is a book about UWL and not a book specifically about SAP Business Workflow, although workflow integration does form a large part of the content. Rather than using a lot of different workflows then, the same demonstration workflow, WS30000015, is used throughout. This is a standard SAP-provided workflow that models the sce-

nario of an employee requesting a leave of absence from his manager.

The examples run on two servers: a SAP NetWeaver Portal 7.0 SP9 instance on *http://portal.fortybeans.com: 50000* and a SAP NetWeaver 7.0 SP12 ABAP instance on *workflow.fortybeans.com*. Each of these is based on the corresponding SAP NetWeaver Sneak Preview, which you can download from the SAP Community Network at *http://sdn.sap.com*.

Acknowledgements

Writing a book while doing a full-time job is not an easy thing and would not have been possible at all without the help and support of several people. First and foremost, my wife Alina has given up nearly a year's worth of weekends to support me during the writing process, and she has been instrumental in curtailing the worst excesses of my procrastination. Thanks are also due to my mother and brother for being a great family.

My editor, Stefan Proksch, and all the staff at Galileo Press have shown faith in my ability to produce the book and have done much to improve its quality and get it published in good time (in spite of my grossly underestimating the effort involved). From SAP, Jocelyn Dart provided excellent feedback during the technical review, and both Alan Rickayzen and Ginger Gatling provided important encouragement and feedback earlier on in the book's gestation.

Finally, I would like to thank my employer Axon Solutions for providing me with the opportunity to gain an in-depth understanding of the Universal Worklist's use in the field, which was the motivation for writing the book in the first place.

2 Standard Universal Worklist Configuration

In this chapter, you're going to learn two things. First, you'll see how easy it is to get the Universal Worklist (UWL) working with an SAP Business Workflow back end (see Section 2.1). Next, you'll see how UWL is configured (see Section 2.2) and how to use this configuration to change the UWL's layout (see Section 2.3) and to control what happens when users click on a work item (see Section 2.4). These make up the most common activities on any project involving UWL.

The nerve center for UWL configuration is in the SAP NetWeaver Portal (called "the portal" from now on) at **System Administration • System Configuration • Universal Worklist & Workflow • Universal Worklist – Administration** (see Figure 2.1).

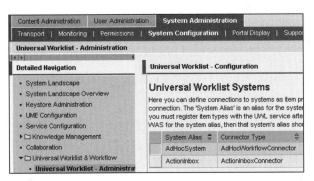

Figure 2.1 Where to Find UWL Configuration in the SAP NetWeaver Portal

UWL comes configured out of the box with two connected systems, both based in the portal. The **AdHocSystem** entry refers to the Ad Hoc workflow feature of the portal (see Section 4.1), which allows users to assign tasks to each other, and the **ActionInbox** entry refers to the workflow used for the approval of documents in the portal's Knowledge Management (KM) component (see Section 4.2). These system entries are special cases and hard-coded; you can't create new systems with these types,

and you shouldn't change the system types of these entries.

2.1 Connecting SAP Systems

Most of the time, the first thing you will want to do with UWL is to connect it to an ABAP-based system so you can bring work items from SAP Business Workflow through to the portal. This is particularly important when you are using the portal to access more than one SAP system's workflow — users don't want to have to log into one system (SAP SRM) to approve purchase requisitions and then log in to another system (SAP ERP) to approve the resulting invoices for payment. In this section, you'll see how to set up connections to a workflow system and find out some of the things you have to look out for when you're configuring the system.

Throughout this section, we'll set up a connection to client 100 of a SAP Business Workflow system NSP (a SAP NetWeaver Trial Version instance), which is system number 00 and whose web interface is accessed with the URL *http://workflow.fortybeans.com:8000*.

Portal System Definitions

You need to create an entry in the Portal System Landscape[1] entry for each back end system that you want to get work items from by going to the menu **System Administration • System Configuration • System Landscape**; right-clicking in the Portal Content Directory (PCD) on the desired location for the system entry; and selecting **New • System (from template)**, as shown in Figure 2.2.

---

1 Note that the Portal System Landscape is *not* the same as the SAP NetWeaver System Landscape Directory (SLD).

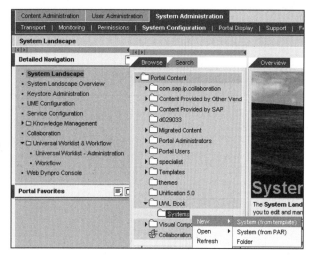

Figure 2.2   Create a System Definition in the Portal's System Landscape

There are three types of system entry you can use:

▶ SAP system using dedicated application server
▶ SAP system with load balancing
▶ SAP system using connection string

The property categories you need to fill in to work with UWL are **Connector** (which is used to get the work items from the back end), **ITS** (to launch back end-based task handlers using the default SAP GUI for HTML or IACs [Internet Application Component][2]), and **WAS** (for task handlers using BSP (Business Server Pages) technology or Web Dynpro). We'll start by looking at the different ways of setting up connectors (depending on the type of system entry you choose) and then we'll move on to setting up **ITS** and **WAS** property categories.

Choosing the Right Kind of System Definition

The template you choose primarily depends on how the portal to back end communication works for fetching work items. The simplest one to set up for development and testing purposes is usually the **SAP system using dedicated application server** template. For productive use, the **SAP system with load balancing** template will often be the most suitable.

---

[2] You can find more information on IACs in the SAP Help Portal at **ITS Administrator's Guide • Internet Transaction Server (ITS) • Internet Application Component (IAC).**

If you have configured the UWL to launch back end task handlers using the SAP GUI for Windows (see "SAP GUI – Win, Web, or Java" in Section 2.4), and your users access the back end system via a SAProuter connection, then you will probably want to use a **SAP system using connection string** template.

Connector Settings

Figure 2.3 to Figure 2.5 show examples of the minimum information necessary to establish a connection for each of the three templates. Here are the settings you need to use[3]:

▶ **SAP system using dedicated application server**
  ▶ **Application host**: The host name or IP address of the SAP Business Workflow system, as seen from the portal server.
  ▶ **SAP Client**: The workflow system's client number.
  ▶ **SAP System ID (SID)**
  ▶ **SAP System Number**
  ▶ **System Type**: Usually **SAP_R3** unless this is a BW or CRM (customer relationship management) system, in which case **SAP_BW** or **SAP_CRM**, respectively.

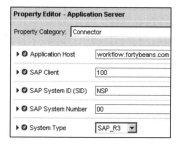

Figure 2.3   Minimal Settings for a Dedicated Application Server

▶ **SAP system with load balancing:**
  ▶ **Group**: The login group (of application servers) to use
  ▶ **Message Server**: The host name or IP address of the SAP Business Workflow system's message server, as seen from the portal server.
  ▶ **SAP Client**: The workflow system's client number.
  ▶ **SAP System ID (SID)**
  ▶ **SAP System Number**

---

[3] You may need to talk to your friendly local Basis administrator to get all of these settings.

▶ **System Type**: Usually **SAP_R3** unless this is a BW or CRM system, in which case **SAP_BW** or **SAP_CRM**, respectively.

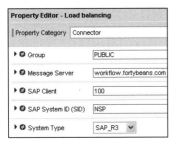

Figure 2.4   Minimal Settings for Load Balancing

▶ **SAP system using connection string:**

   ▶ **Connection String to Application**: The connection string to use to get to the workflow system via a SAP router.[4]

   ▶ **SAP Client**: The workflow system's client number.

   ▶ **SAP System ID (SID)**

   ▶ **SAP System Number**

   ▶ **System Type**: Usually **SAP_R3** unless this is a BW or CRM system, in which case **SAP_BW** or **SAP_CRM**, respectively.

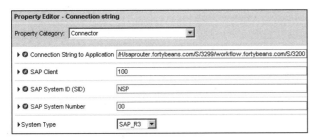

Figure 2.5   Minimal Settings for Connection String

ITS and WAS settings

After the **Connector** properties are correctly defined, then you need to configure the web access sections. SAP GUI for HTML and IACs use the **Internet Transaction Server (ITS)** section (see Figure 2.6); Web Dynpro and BSP components use the **Web Application Server (Web AS)** section (see Figure 2.7). These property categories are set up almost identically, using the same values for the **Host Name** and **Protocol** fields.

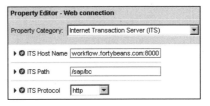

Figure 2.6   Settings for ITS

The **Host Name** field is the host name and port of the SAP Business Workflow server as seen by the user's browser, as opposed to the **Connector** setting discussed previously, which is the name of the server as seen from the portal server. The **Protocol** field determines whether the user's browser uses HTTP or HTTPS as the protocol to access the SAP Business Workflow server. An HTTPS connection is strongly recommended for production situations, for security reasons.

Figure 2.7   Settings for Web AS

The only field that differs between the two categories is the **Path** field, which is set to /sap/bc for the **ITS Path** and /sap for the **Web AS Path** (although it turns out that in most cases, the values of **Path** are actually ignored by the portal).

UWL System Definitions

Now you've set up the definition of the system you want to connect to, the next step is to make UWL aware of it.

The first step is to assign a *system alias*, or nickname for the system. If you don't do this, then the system won't be available for selection when you're setting up UWL. System aliases are what the portal components use to refer to system entries.

1. To assign a system alias to a portal system, select **System Aliases** from the **Display** drop-down menu when you're editing that system in the portal (see Figure 2.8). This will take you to the System Alias editor.

---

4 See the SAP Help Portal on connection strings at **SAProuter • Using SAProuter • Route Strings**.

Figure 2.8   Selecting System Aliases from the Display Dropdown

2. In the **System Alias Editor** (see Figure 2.9), you need to enter at least one alias. The first alias you enter becomes the *default alias*[5]. In the example shown, the alias `SAP_R3_Workflow` is about to be added to a system that already has a default alias of `NSP_100`. Click the **Save** button when you're done entering aliases.

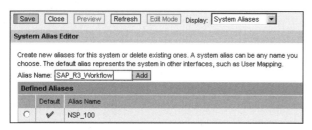

Figure 2.9   The System Alias Editor

3. Select **Permissions** from the **Display** dropdown and make sure that end users have at least **Read** permissions, with the **End User** box checked, for the system entry in the portal (see Figure 2.10). Figure 2.10 shows the simple option of giving **Everyone** access; in a more restrictive security environment, you may want to be more specific about which portal roles are allowed access to the system (although even with **Everyone** given access, users are still restricted in what they can do in that system by the security roles assigned in the back end itself). Make sure to click the **Save** button when you've defined the permissions.

4. Navigate to **System Administration • System Configuration • Universal Worklist & Workflow • Universal Worklist – Administration,** and click on the **New** button to start the process of connecting UWL to the system you've just defined (see Figure 2.11).

5. In the resulting form, enter a **System Alias** of the system you're connecting to UWL. Leave the **Connector Type** set to **WebFlowConnector**, leave the other entries at their default or empty values for now, and then click **Save** (see Figure 2.12).

---

5 The default alias is the one used for setting up User Mapping, a single sign-on method that is beyond the scope of this book.

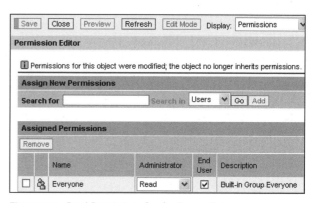

Figure 2.10   Read Permissions for the System Entry

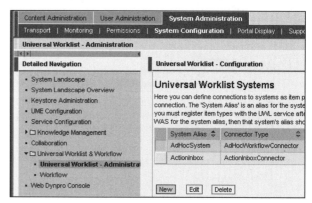

Figure 2.11   Universal Worklist Systems Screen

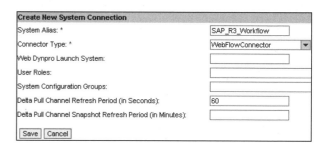

Figure 2.12   UWL Systems Definition

6. The newly defined system (**SAP_R3_Workflow**) will then appear in the list of UWL systems.

SAP Authorizations and Prerequisites Needed for UWL

Before you actually connect to the back end SAP Business Workflow system, you need to have certain items in place on that system. These are slightly different depending on whether you are using a SAP NetWeaver 2004 or a SAP NetWeaver 7.0 system:

▶ **Common Prerequisites**

   ▶ Users need to have authorization in the SAP Business Workflow system to call Remote Function

Calls (RFC) in function groups SWRC, SDTX, and SSCV.

▸ The back end workflow system must have an active Internet Transaction Server (ITS) enabled.

▸ Workflow has been set up in the SAP Business Workflow system (transaction SWU3).

▸ Single sign-on has been set up from the portal to the SAP Business Workflow system.

▸ **SAP NetWeaver 2004 Prerequisites**

▸ Either Content Management must be installed, or the instructions in SAP Note 702255 must be followed.

▸ Users must have authorizations to call RFCs in function group SWK1 and also to run transaction SWK1.

▸ Workplace plug-in 6.0 must be installed on the back end workflow system.

▸ **SAP NetWeaver 7.0 Prerequisites**

▸ See SAP Note 941589 for the roles required by UWL administrators and end users in the workflow system.

▸ Users also need authorization to call RFCs in function group SWN_UWL_WL.

Registering Item Types

The final step in getting the UWL up and running is to tell it about all the different kinds of work items in the back end and what to do when a user clicks on each type of work item. The easiest way to do this is to pull down a list of task definitions from the back end system; we'll look at how to customize the launch behavior later in Section 2.4.

The downloading of this configuration from the back end is called *registration* and is achieved by clicking the **Register** button in the list of UWL systems, as shown in Figure 2.13. It may take several minutes to download the item type configuration from the back end.

System Alias	Connector Type	Action	Activate Connection
AdHocSystem	AdHocWorkflowConnector		Deactivate
ActionInbox	ActionInboxConnector		Deactivate
SAP_R3_Workflow	WebFlowConnector	Register	Deactivate

Figure 2.13 UWL Systems List

If you make any changes in the back end, for example changing the workflow configuration or changing the UWL customization in transaction SWFVISU (see Section

2.4), then you must come back to the UWL systems list and click the **Re-Register** button.

Configuring Alerts

To configure the UWL to receive messages from the SAP Alert Framework, just create an entry in exactly the same way as described previously (you can use the same **System Alias** name), but choose **AlertConnector** instead of **WebFlowConnector**.

You can find documentation on configuring the Alert Management Framework in the SAP Help Portal (*http://help.sap.com*) in the category **Alert Management (BC-SRV-GBT-ALM)**.

The Result

Now you've set up UWL to talk to an SAP Business Workflow system. To prove that it all works, you'll want to kick off a sample workflow and see the resulting work item appear in the portal by following these steps:

1. Log in to the SAP Business Workflow system, and run transaction SWU3. This is the transaction used to set up the workflow system (see Appendix A for details), and assuming the system has been set up correctly, you should see a list of green ticks. Don't worry if the **Guided Procedures** entry has a red cross: this is only needed for connecting the SAP Business Workflow to Guided Procedures (more details in Chapter 4). You can see what this transaction looks like in Figure 2.14.

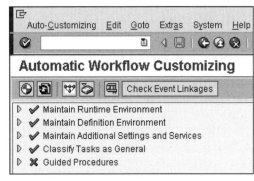

Figure 2.14 Transaction SWU3 Showing a Mostly Set Up SAP Business Workflow System

2. If you click on the icon (**Start verification workflow**), this will start a simple workflow. You can check that this has worked by clicking on the icon (**SAP Business Workplace**), which takes you to the SAP

Inbox. Select the **Workflow** category, and you should see a work item titled **First step in workflow verification** (see Figure 2.15).

Figure 2.15 SAP Inbox Showing the Work Item from the Verification Workflow

3. As a final step to check that everything is set up correctly, log in to the portal, and navigate to UWL. Assuming you have the Standard User role `pcd:por-`

`tal_content/every_user/general/eu_role` this will be at **Home • Work • Overview**.

4. If everything has gone to plan, you should see a screen that looks something like Figure 2.16, with a work item titled **First step in workflow verification**.

2.2 Overview of UWL Configuration

Now you've learned how to get UWL working with an SAP Business Workflow system. Before you find out how to change the appearance and behavior of UWL, let's first look at the different methods of configuration.

UWL is configured using four main mechanisms:

▶ Setting property values on the UWL iView
▶ Using the available UWL configuration wizards
▶ Hand-editing an XML configuration file
▶ Using transaction SWFVISU in the SAP Business Workflow system

The next sections look at each of these options in turn.

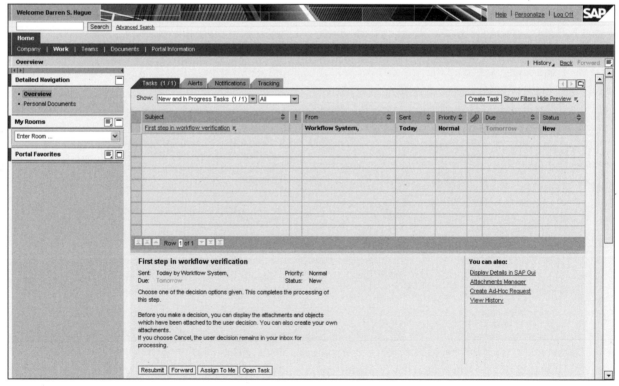

Figure 2.16 UWL Showing a Work Item from a SAP Business Workflow System

Seeing the Effect of Changes

If you have an end user logged in to the portal when you are making changes to UWL configuration, that user may have to log out and log in again to see the effect of those changes.

iView Properties

The default UWL iView used in the SAP-provided worksets is in the PCD at **Portal Content • Content Provided by SAP • End User Content • Standard Portal Users • iViews • com.sap.coll.iviews • Universal Worklist** (pcd:portal_content/com.sap.pct/every_user/general/iViews/com.sap.coll.iviews/com.sap.netweaver.coll.uwl.uwl_iview), but if you want to change any of the properties for your own customizations, then it is highly recommended to create a delta-linked copy of this iView in a customer-specific PCD location. If you make any changes to the default UWL iView, then you will lose them the next time a support package is installed; by using a delta-linked copy, your customizations are preserved, but you will still inherit any new or changed properties that appear in a new version of the iView.

Wizards

There are a number of wizards to help with the following tasks:

▶ Customizing the look of the UWL main page
▶ Customizing the appearance of work items
▶ Customizing the launch behavior of work items

These wizards create XML configuration files (see the next section, "XML Configuration") for you, making it much simpler to do certain kinds of configuration. You can also use these generated XML files as the basis for further customization.

XML Configuration

Most of the detailed configuration on UWL is done by creating and uploading XML configuration files. The syntax of these files can be found in the SAP Help Portal at **Business Task Management • Universal Worklist Configuration • Configuration DTD**.

When XML configuration files are uploaded into the portal, you specify whether the task customizations are adjusted for one specific UWL system or whether they apply to all systems (e.g., when specifying the visual layout in UWL), that is, whether the references in the file are system-specific or global in nature. You also specify whether the priority of the file is **Medium** (default) or **High** (see Figure 2.17 for an example of the configuration upload screen). When you register the item types from a back end system (see "Registering Item Types" in Section 2.1), this creates an XML configuration of priority **Low**, so your customizations will always override what was read from the back end.

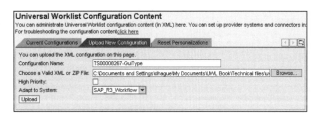

Figure 2.17   Uploading a New XML Configuration

To upload a new XML configuration, navigate to **System Administration • System Configuration • Universal Worklist & Workflow • Universal Worklist - Administration**, and then click the link **Click to Administrate Item Types and View Definitions**. On the next screen, select the **Upload New Configuration** tab.

Fill in the name of the configuration (to ease maintenance, this should be similar to the name of the XML file), select a system if you are doing a system-specific customization, check the **High Priority** box if required[6], and then click **Upload**.

Transaction SWFVISU in the SAP Business Workflow System

Some basic customizing of how a task is launched can be done in the SAP Business Workflow system using transaction SWFVISU (discussed in more detail in Section 2.4). Any such customizations will be downloaded to the portal when you register the item types (see "Registering Item Types" in Section 2.1), but like any UWL configura-

---

6 You should usually upload with priority **Medium** (the default), leaving **High** for special cases (e.g., you have a **Medium**-level customization for all systems, but you have a specific exception for one system, which should go in as priority **High**). You can also use **High** for testing new configurations without changing the original XML file, by simply overriding it for the new settings.

tion downloaded from the SAP Business Workflow system, the priority of these customizations is **Low**, meaning that they will be overridden by any customization you carry out using the methods described previously in Section 2.2.

2.3 Changing the Basic Look of UWL

In SAP NetWeaver Portal 7.0, it has become much easier to change the look and feel of UWL than in previous releases. The underlying configuration is the same — namely creating and editing entries in an XML file — but now there are some wizards to generate the XML for you in some cases.

Clearing the Cache

Whenever you carry out any customization of UWL, it's a good idea to clear the UWL caches afterwards to make sure your configuration applies to all items. Failure to do this can lead to confusion as items appear in their pre-change state due to remaining in the cache.

You can clear the caches by navigating to **System Administration • System Configuration • Universal Worklist & Workflow • Universal Worklist - Administration** and then clicking the link **Cache Administration Page** in the section **Universal Worklist Content Configuration**.

Changing the Look of the Worklist

The first thing you're going to learn to change is the appearance of the list of work items. You can do this either by using the provided wizard (see the following section, "Basic Configuration") or by creating a UWL XML file (see the following Section, "Expert Configuration").

Basic Configuration

If you just want to change the ordering and visibility of the UWL tabs or columns in the default iView for all users, you can use the wizard-based configuration in the portal.

1. Navigate to **System Administration • System Configuration • Universal Worklist & Workflow • Universal Worklist – Administration**, look for the heading **Universal Worklist Content Configuration**, and click on

Click to Configure Item Types and Customize Views Using a Wizard (the link highlighted in Figure 2.18).

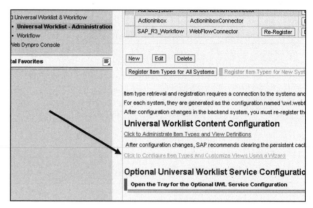

Figure 2.18 Link to Wizard-Based Configuration

2. On the resulting page, select the option **Customize the look of the UWL main page**, and click **Next**. You will then see the **Navigation Node Configuration** screen, a simulation of the UWL look and feel that allows you to modify dynamically the visibility and ordering of tabs (see Figure 2.19).

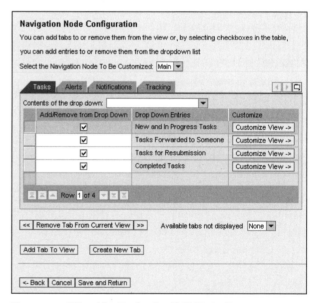

Figure 2.19 Wizard for Configuring UWL Navigation

For example, if you want to focus your users' attention entirely on their current workflow tasks by removing the other tabs, you should select each of the tabs **Alerts**, **Notifications**, and **Tracking**.

3. After selecting each tab, click the button **Remove Tab From Current View**. When you've removed those

three tabs, click the **Save and Return** button. You can see the effect on UWL for the end user in Figure 2.20 and Figure 2.21.

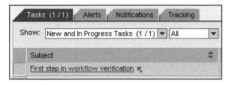

Figure 2.20 Before Removing Tabs

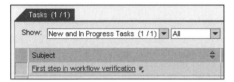

Figure 2.21 After Removing Tabs

Now that you have seen how to control which tabs are displayed, the next task is to change the columns that are displayed within each tab.

1. Go to the **Navigation Node Configuration** screen again (see the beginning of this section for how to find it).

2. Change the layout of the work items in the list of **New and In Progress Tasks** (the other entries work in the same way). Select that row, and click the **Customize View** button; this gives you a screen similar to the one a user gets when selecting the **Personalize view** option, and allows many aspects of the columns and rows to be customized.

3. The first section of the customizing screen (see Figure 2.22) lets you move columns around, delete columns,

and add new columns from those available in the dropdown list.[7] If your users find the standard terminology confusing, you can even rename the column titles.

4. For each column, you can also select the alignment (**Center**, **Left**, **Right,** and **Justify**) and the column width. For columns showing a date, you can also choose whether to show just the date, just the time, or both the date and the time together, and how the date is shown (see Table 2.1).

Date Format Setting	Appearance of Date and Time
Short	3/14/07 9:30 PM
Medium	Mar 14, 2007 9:30 PM
Long	March 14, 2007 9:34:40 PM GMT
Full	Wednesday, March 14, 2007 9:34:40 PM GMT

Table 2.1 Date Format Settings

5. The next section of the customizing screen (see Figure 2.23) lets you control how the columns are sorted. You can choose up to three columns; items are sorted by the first column first, and then by the second column where there are entries with the same value for the first column, and finally by the third column if

---

7 The list of attributes available depends on the list you are customizing and can even include attributes that you have defined. See Section 3.1 for more details.

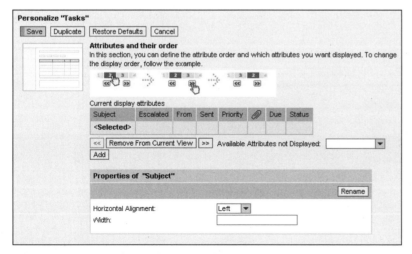

Figure 2.22 Column Ordering, Alignment, and Size

there are entries with the same values for the first and second columns.

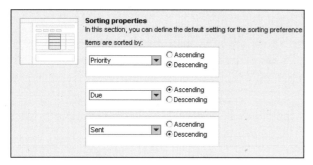

Figure 2.23   Defining How Columns Are Sorted

> **Hint**
>
> Experience shows that many users prefer work items to be sorted like their emails, with the most recent at the top (i.e., **Sent**, **Descending** as the first entry), as opposed to the default ordering, which sorts first by priority, then by due date, and finally by sent date.

6. The third section of the customizing screen (see Figure 2.24) lets you dictate how many work items appear per page, how often the page is refreshed (i.e., how often the back end workflow system is checked for fresh data), how long before the due date it is before items are flagged as **Warning** or **Severe**, and whether rows are shown in alternating colors, or just in one color.

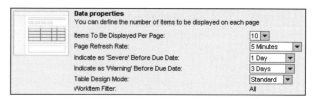

Figure 2.24   General Data Properties

7. The final section of the customizing screen (see Figure 2.25) lets you control whether the header and footer of the worklist are displayed. The footer contains the page up/page down navigation controls, and is usually displayed. The header contains the same text as the tab name and is therefore usually not displayed.

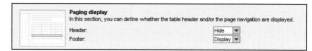

Figure 2.25   Header and Footer Display

8. When you have finished customizing the layout in the four parts of the **Customize View** screen, clicking **Save** and then **Save and Return** causes the portal to create a new custom XML configuration file on your behalf, storing it in the portal with priority **High**, so that it overrides any existing configuration (see Figure 2.26).

You can use this wizard just as it is, or you can use it as the basis for generating a new XML configuration file that you can then fine-tune manually using the following section, "Expert Configuration," as a guide. If you do decide

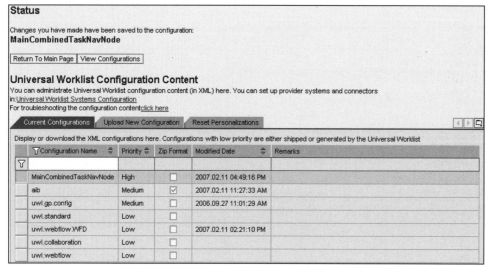

Figure 2.26   New Configuration Entry, MainCombinedTaskNavNode, as Created by the Wizard

to do that, then after you have downloaded the generated XML, you should delete the wizard-generated entry from the configuration list; otherwise, its priority of **High** will not let any of your XML customizations show.

Expert Configuration

When navigating to the UWL from the **Home • Work • Overview** path (in the Standard User Role[8]), the tabs shown by default are determined by two properties of the UWL iView (useNavigationId and sap_uwl_viewname) and some XML configuration.

The property useNavigationId on the UWL iView points to a section of the XML configuration file. In the standard iView, this property is set to the value Main and

corresponds to the following configuration fragment in the uwl.standard XML configuration (see Listing 2.1).

As you can see, this XML fragment contains a NavigationNode element for each tab. The **Tasks** tab is selected by default, determined by the iView property sap_uwl_viewname having the default value DefaultView.

Example of UWL Navigation Tab Customizing

For example, if you want a specialized UWL iView with only **Tasks** and **Notifications** tabs being shown and **Notifications** to be selected by default, you would do the following:

1. Copy the XML fragment for NavigationNode Main from *uwl.standard.xml* and paste into a new file, say *uwl.customnavigation.xml*.

2. Change the name property of the top-level NavigationNode to (for example) MyCustom:

---

8 This role includes the **Overview** page (via some worksets) at pcd:portal_content/com.sap.pct/every_user/general/pages/com.sap.km.pages/com.sap.km.Overview, and the Overview page includes the UWL iView pcd:portal_content/com.sap.pct/every_user/general/iViews/com.sap.coll.iviews/com.sap.netweaver.coll.uwl.uwl_iview.

```
<NavigationNode name="Main" view="" referenceGroup="" visible="yes"
 keepItemCountUpdated="no">

  <NavigationNode name="CombinedTask" view="DefaultView" referenceGroup=""
   visible="yes" keepItemCountUpdated="no" referenceBundle="tasks">

    ...

  </NavigationNode>

  <NavigationNode name="alert2" view="AlertsView" referenceGroup="" visible="yes"
   keepItemCountUpdated="no" referenceBundle="alerts">

    ...

  </NavigationNode>

  <NavigationNode name="notification2" view="NotificationsView" referenceGroup=""
   visible="yes" keepItemCountUpdated="no" referenceBundle="notifications">

    ...

  </NavigationNode>

  <NavigationNode name="CombinedTracking" view="ComboWorkItemRequestsView"
   referenceGroup="" visible="yes" keepItemCountUpdated="no"
   referenceBundle="tracking">

    ...

  </NavigationNode>
</NavigationNode>
```

Listing 2.1 Standard UWL XML Configuration for Tabs and Their Contents

```
<NavigationNode name="MyCustom"
   view="" referenceGroup=""
   visible="yes" keepItemCountUpdated="no">
```

3. Remove the XML nodes for Alerts and Tracking:

```
<!--NavigationNode name="alert2"
   view="AlertsView" referenceGroup=""
   visible="yes" keepItemCountUpdated="no"
   referenceBundle="alerts">

   ...

</NavigationNode-->
```

4. Save this file, and upload it into the portal (see "XML Configuration" in Section 2.2) with priority **Medium** or **High**.

5. Create a delta-linked copy of the UWL iView in your own area of the PCD.[9]

6. On your copy of the iView, set the property useNavigationId to MyCustom and set the property sap_uwl_viewname to NotificationsView.

Now you can assign this iView to the page, workset, or role of your choice in the portal.

Which Buttons and Links Are Shown

You can hide almost any of the buttons and actions in the UWL that you do not want users to see. This is done by setting the **List of UWL Actions to exclude** property (excludeActionList) on the UWL iView.

The list of available actions is shown in Table 2.2 (from the SAP Help Portal at **Business Task Management • Advanced Configuration • Removing Actions From the UWL Display**).

For example, your organization may take the view that being able to launch a SAP GUI to see work item details or being able to personalize the layout of UWL, are actions that might confuse users who rarely use SAP and may lead to too many calls to the help desk. In this case, you would replace the standard UWL iView with your delta-linked copy[10], with the **List of UWL Actions to**

---

9 Creating a delta-linked copy of SAP standard content means that your iView will survive any future portal upgrades while inheriting any new properties that may be added in future releases.

10 See Section iView Properties for more details on creating a delta-linked UWL iView.

---

exclude property set to personalize, launchSAPDetails (see Figure 2.27).

Figure 2.27   Removing the Ability to Personalize UWL and Launch SAP GUI

Action Display Text	Action Name
Alerts	AlertConfiguration
Claim	reserve
Complete	acknowledge
Complete Task	confirm
Create Ad Hoc Request	uwlTaskWizard
Create Task	defaultGlobalWizard
Decline	decline
Delete	deleteItem
Edit	editItem
Follow-up	followUp
Forward	forward
Forward	forwardUsers (this action is for multiple user selection)
Manage Attachments	manageAttachments
Open Task	launchSAPAction
Personalize View	personalize
Revoke Claim	replace
Submit Memo	addmemo
View Detail in SAP GUI	launchSAPDetails

Table 2.2   UWL Elements That Can Be Hidden with excludeActions

Which Details Are Shown

The details shown for a work item in the preview area (and whether the preview area is shown at all) can also be configured by setting properties on the UWL iView.

The UWL property **List of preview sections to hide** (excludePreviewSections) can take a comma-separated list of the following values: SUBJECT, ATTRIBUTES,

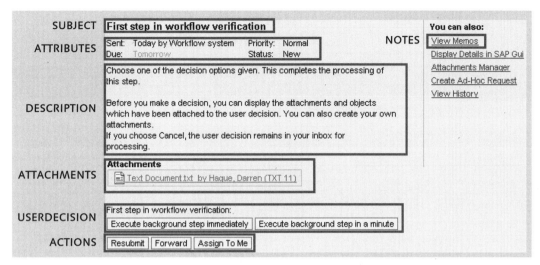

Figure 2.28   Which Parts of the UWL Item Details Are Hidden with Each excludePreviewSections Value

DESCRIPTION, ATTACHMENTS, NOTES[11], USERDECISION, and/or ACTIONS. You can see in Figure 2.28 how these values correspond to the various parts of the work item details screen. Each attribute you add to the list will result in that part of the screen not being shown.

You can control the other parts of the screen (**Display Details in SAP Gui**, **Attachments Manager**, and **Create Ad-Hoc Request**) using the excludeActionList configuration in the previous section. In fact, the only item in the work item detail screen that cannot be hidden from view is the **View History** link.

Attached Business Objects

In the previous section, "Which Details are Shown," you saw how to hide all attachments using the parameter ATTACHMENTS for the UWL iView property excludeActionList. This section explains how to control attachment display in a more fine-grained manner from the back end, when the attachments relate to the display of business objects such as the FORMABSENC object (used as the basis of the Absence Notification workflow in the rest of this book).

You can hide attached business objects in UWL work items or even replace the standard attachment call with your own application using the **Object Visualization** section of transaction SWFVISU. Leaving the **Method Name**

blank and setting the **Visualization Type** to **Object Not Represented** will hide the attachment completely (see Figure 2.29). Any other visualization type means that the attachment will link to the specified application rather than the default method for that object, for example, to a Web Dynpro application that gives a summary of the requested absence.

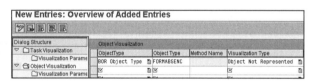

Figure 2.29   Using SWFVISU to Hide FORMABSENC Object Attachments

Substitution

This section looks at how to control end users' access to the substitution functionality of UWL. Users can choose other people to fill in for them while they are on leave or ill; by choosing a substitute in this way, all of the original user's tasks will appear in the substitute's worklist (as long as the substitute agrees to take on this responsibility). The original user accesses the screens for setting up substitution by selecting **Manage Substitution Rules** from the context menu of UWL (see Figure 2.30).

If you don't want to let your users set up (or even view) substitutes in this way, you can hide the menu item by setting the UWL iView property **Display substituted user selector** to **No**.

---

11   NOTES corresponds to the **View Memos** link. Memos are simply plain text attachments that have been created via the SAP Inbox as type RAW.

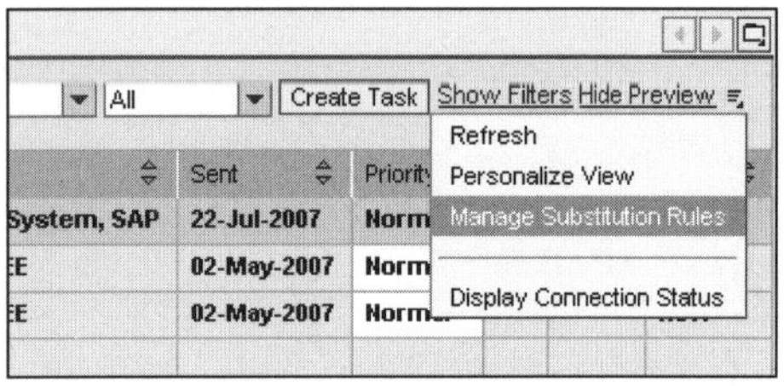

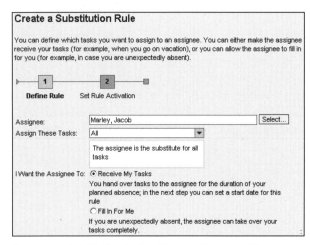

Figure 2.30   Context Menu Item for Managing Substitutes

For more fine-grained control over how your users perform substitutions, go to the UWL iView property category **UWL Substitutions**, which gives you four settings:

▶ **Disable Substitution Profiles**
With this property set to the default of **No**, users can choose which types of task can be seen by their substitute (see Figure 2.31). When the property is set to **Yes**, users do not get this control, and their substitutes get all their tasks.

Figure 2.31   Substitution Profiles Shown in Dropdown Menu

▶ **Disable Turn On/Off buttons**
Setting this property to **Yes** will remove the buttons that allow a user to enable and disable each substitution rule (the column labeled **1** in Figure 2.32).

▶ **Display Create/Delete buttons**
Setting this property to **No** will remove the **Create Rule** and **Delete** buttons (labeled **2** in Figure 2.32). This effectively removes users' ability to set up substitutions but leaves them able to view existing ones.

▶ **Hide Rule Activation Column**
Setting this property to **Yes** will hide the column **Rule Activation** from view (labeled **3** in Figure 2.32) so that

users will not be able to see if their rules were activated successfully or not. You might do this if you have a back end system that does not fully support substitution — users might see a confusing error message even if there is nothing to worry about.

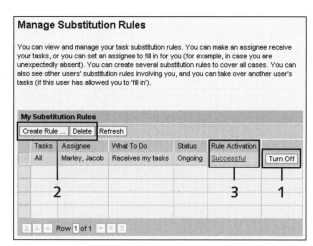

Figure 2.32   Options for UWL Substitutions Display

Debugging Information
You can get some really useful debugging information by setting the UWL iView property **Display UWL Support Information** (technical name `displaySupport`) to **Yes**.

2.4   How Work Items Are Launched

Up to this point, you've seen how to get UWL working with an SAP Business Workflow system and how to control what it looks like onscreen. Now it's time to look at controlling what happens when a user clicks on one of the items in the worklist.

When a user clicks on an item in UWL, an *action handler* is invoked to deal with that item. There is a whole range of possible action handlers (see Table 2.3[12]), but here we'll only look at some of the more common options.

---

12 This list is taken from the SAP Help Portal at **Business Task Management • Universal Worklist Configuration • Advanced Configuration • Task Launch Customization • Action Handlers**.

Action Handler Name	Description
IviewLauncher	Launches a portal iView or page
SAPAppLauncher	Launches a portal iView based on a BSP, IAC, MiniApp, transaction, or Web Dynpro
SAPMiniAppLauncher	Launches an old-style SAP MiniApp (for ITS versions older than 6.40)
SAPIACLauncher	Launches an ITS IAC or MiniApp
SAPWebDynproLauncher	Launches a Web Dynpro Java application
SAPWebDynproABAPLauncher	Launches a Web Dynpro ABAP application
SAPTransactionLauncher	Launches a SAP transaction using SAP GUI (HTML, Windows, or Java)
SAPBSPLauncher	Launches a BSP application
ObjectLinkLauncher	Launches a BSP for the corresponding CRM object type
ObjectNavigationLauncher	Launches a portal iView or page for an ABAP business object
UrlLauncher	Launches a web page
XhandlerLauncher	Consults a back end SAP Business Workflow system for the handler to launch
TerminatingEventHandler	Runs a terminating event handler in a back end SAP Business Workflow system
FunctionModuleActionHandler	Runs a function module in a back end SAP Business Workflow system
UpdatingContainerHandler	Writes data back to the workflow container in a back end SAP system
UserDecisionHandler	Writes the user's decision on a decision workflow item to a back end SAP system
PortalEventLauncher	Fires a portal event

Table 2.3   Action Handlers and What They Do

SAP GUI — Win, Web, or Java

If you use the SAPTransactionLauncher action handler, a SAP GUI session will be launched and (if no specific TransactionCode parameter is used) will behave in the same way as if the user had clicked on the item in the SAP Business Workplace (transaction SBWP).

By default, the SAP GUI for HTML (Web GUI) is used for these transactions, but this is not always the most appropriate option (see Chapter 5 for a discussion of the issues to consider when choosing which version of SAP GUI to use). Therefore, you may need to deploy SAP GUI for Windows or SAP GUI for Java to your UWL users, and you will then want to configure UWL to launch a Windows or Java GUI. There are two alternatives here: you can configure UWL to launch a different GUI for all item types, or you can do it just for the individual item types you care about.

Configuring a GUI for All Item Types

To configure UWL to launch a different GUI type for all items, you need to create a custom version of the UWL iView, **UWL – Launch SAP Transaction**[13] at pcd:portal_content/every_user/general/uwl/com.sap.netweaver.bc.uwl.uwlSapLaunch. The quick-and-dirty way to do this is by making a simple change to the SAP-provided version of the iView, as shown in Figure 2.33: Change the **SAP GUI Type** property to **SAP GUI for Windows**.

Of course, it can be dangerous to make changes to SAP-standard content because these changes are likely to be overwritten the next time a support package or upgrade is applied. A better way to make the customization is to create delta-linked copies of the UWL iViews shown previously to a new folder in a customer-specific space and make your changes to the copied version of the iView. That way, your changes will not be overwritten by

---

13 The complete path for this iView is **Portal Content/Portal Users/Standard Portal Users/Universal Worklist/UWL – Launch SAP Transaction**.

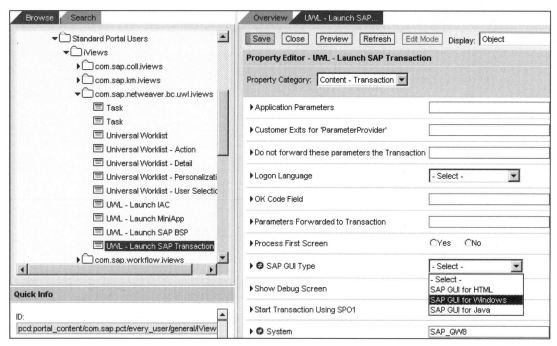

Figure 2.33   Changing the GUI Type for All UWL Items

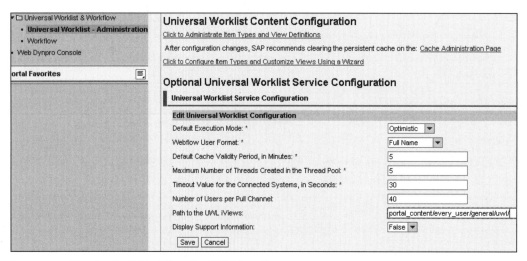

Figure 2.34   Changing the Folder Where the UWL iViews Live

an upgrade, but because of delta-linking, your iView will always be based on the latest version of the SAP iView in the original folder.

If you do go down the route of creating delta-linked copies, you need to tell UWL to use your new folder for these iViews instead of the original folder. You can do this by navigating to **System Administration • System Config-uration • Universal Worklist & Workflow • Universal Worklist - Administration** and then clicking the icon to expand the section **Optional Universal Worklist Service**

Configuration. Click the **Edit** button, and then, as shown in Figure 2.34, change the property `Path to the UWL iViews` from `portal_content/every_user/general/uwl/` to the PCD URL of your customer-specific folder[14] (don't forget the trailing /). Click **Save** to finish.

---

14 You can get the PCD location of a folder by opening that folder as an object in the portal PCD editor (**Content Admin-istration • Portal Content**). The PCD location is the value of the **PCD location** property but without the `pcd:` at the front.

Launching a Windows SAP GUI from UWL

Bear in mind that the same system landscape entry in the portal is used both for fetching work items from the back end to the portal and also for launching SAP GUI task handlers for work items. In other words, the portal server must be able to access the SAP Business Workflow server in the same way as an end-user's PC.

This may not always be easy; for example, it is quite common for SAP GUI users to access the back end server via a SAProuter connection for security reasons, but the portal may be configured for a direct connection. The solution is to configure the SAProuter instance to allow two routes through to the back end: one from the portal server and one from the network where your users' SAP GUI sessions are running and then create a system landscape entry of type **SAP system using connection string** for UWL use.

Note that the SAProuter instance must be accessible using the same host name from both your client network and your SAP server network.

Configuring a GUI for Specific Item Types
The default SAP GUI for HTML may be fine for most of your users, but it may be that for one specific type of work item, a SAP GUI for Windows is required.

You can configure an individual work item type to launch a Windows GUI-based handler by creating an XML file like the one in Listing 2.2, replacing TS00008267 with the code for the task type you are interested in. If you don't know the task type, then run transaction SWDD, open the workflow, and double-click on the relevant node to find out; alternatively, ask your local workflow consultant.

You can configure a different GUI by changing the value of the property `GuiType` to `WinGui` or `JavaGui`, according to the type of GUI you want to launch for that task. The XML file should then be uploaded into the portal as described in "XML Configuration" in Section 2.2.

Nonportal URLs
The `UrlLauncher` action handler can be useful when you want to write a work item handler in some web technology otherwise unsupported by UWL, for example, a PHP

```
<?xml version="1.0" encoding="utf-8"?>

<!DOCTYPE UWLConfiguration PUBLIC '- //SAP//UWL1.0//EN' 'uwl_configuration.dtd'>
<UWLConfiguration version="1.0">
  <ItemTypes>
    <ItemType name="uwl.task.webflow.TS00008267" connector="WebFlowConnector"
    defaultView="DefaultView" defaultAction="launchSAPAction"
    executionMode="default">
      <ItemTypeCriteria externalType="TS00008267" connector="WebFlowConnector"/>
      <Actions>
        <Action name="launchSAPAction" handler="SAPTransactionLauncher">
          <Properties>
            <Property name="GuiType" value="WinGui"/>
          </Properties>
        </Action>
      </Actions>
    </ItemType>
  </ItemTypes>
</UWLConfiguration>
```

Listing 2.2   UWL XML Configuration File to Launch TS00008267 (Generic Decision) Tasks Using SAP GUI for Windows (WinGui) script.[15] For example, suppose you have a simple PHP script, *showWorkitemId.php*, which reports the work item ID that is passed to it as the parameter wi_id[16] (see Listing 2.3).

```
<html>
  <head><title>PHP iView</title></head>
  <body>
The workitem ID is
    <?php echo $_GET['wi_id'] ?>.
  </body>
</html>
```
Listing 2.3   Simple PHP Script to Show the Work Item ID

The XML configuration fragment shown in Listing 2.4 shows a button labeled **PHP_Handler** onscreen, which launches the PHP script in a new window when a user clicks on it. The PHP script is launched in a new browser window.

```
<ItemType name="uwl.task.webflow.TS00008267"
  connector="WebFlowConnector"
  defaultView="DefaultView"
  defaultAction="PHP_Handler"
  executionMode="default">
  <ItemTypeCriteria externalType="TS00008267"
    connector="WebFlowConnector"/>
  <Actions>
    <Action name="PHP_Handler"
      handler="UrlLauncher">
      <Properties>
        <Property name="url"
          value="http://phpserver.company.com/
              ShowWorkitemId.php"/>
        <Property name="wi_id"
          value="${item.externalId}"/>
      </Properties>
    </Action>
  </Actions>
</ItemType>
```
Listing 2.4   XML Configuration to Launch PHP Script

15 See *The SAP Developer's Guide to PHP* (SAP PRESS Essentials, 2006) for more details on using PHP with SAP.
16 A more complex script could, for example, call the SAP function module SAP_WAPI_GET_WORKITEM_DETAIL to get more details about the work item.

An alternative to the XML configuration shown in Listing 2.4 is to use the configuration in the SAP Business Workflow system. After doing a one-off configuration in transaction WF_HANDCUST, you need to run transaction WF_EXTSRV to specify a Web Service, generate a matching task, and re-register the system in the UWL administration page.

The advantage of doing it this way is automatic generation of container elements for each parameter, making it simpler to pass URL parameters back and forth to a parent workflow and giving a standard approach to launch/callback from the URL. More details on this approach are in the SAP Help Portal at **SAP Business Workflow • Reference Documentation • Workflow Builder • Using Web Services**.

Portal iViews and Pages
You can trigger any iView or page in the portal to be launched when a user clicks on a work item in UWL. This is useful if the information needed to process a work item comes from several sources; these can be shown as iViews within a page alongside the iView, which allows the user to complete the work item. This "dashboard" page can then be launched when the user clicks on the relevant work item.

The Problem with URL iViews
Although it is theoretically possible to launch URL iViews from UWL, in practice it's not really worthwhile. The problem is that all the useful information that the UWL normally passes as parameters (such as the work item ID) are ignored; URL iViews ignore any parameters passed to them apart from those explicitly configured in the iView definition (see **iViews • Creating iViews • Creating Web-based URL iViews** for details on setting up URL iViews). In other words, it's impossible for a URL iView launched from UWL to know anything useful about the item being launched.

If you need to launch a URL iView, then you should instead consider either using the `UrlLauncher` action handler (see "Nonportal URLs" in Section 2.4) or creating a custom iView using the portal's Application Integrator (see **Portal Development Manual • Core Development Tasks • Connecting to Backend Systems • Application Integrator • Component com.sap.portal.appintegrator.sap.Generic** in the SAP Help Portal).

To configure UWL to launch a portal page for a generic decision task TS00008267, modify the XML configuration file for the item type as shown in Listing 2.5.

The handler attribute for the action is set to `IView-Launcher`, and a single property `iView` is set to the PCD URL of the page.[17]

---

17 The PCD URL is the value of the **PCD Location** property in the **Information** section of the page's property editor.

Now, when the user clicks on a decision work item, the page is launched, and the parameters shown in Table 2.4 are passed to it.

Parameter	Description
`wi_id`	Work item ID in the provider system
`destination`	System alias in the portal system landscape of the provider system
`item_id`	Internal UWL item ID
`task`	Provider task item type
`uname`	Back end user ID for webflow connector, alert connector, and generic ABAP connector, otherwise, portal user ID
`langu`	User language in uppercase ISO language code

Table 2.4 Parameters Passed by Default to IViewLauncher iViews and Pages

```
<?xml version="1.0" encoding="utf-8"?>

<!DOCTYPE UWLConfiguration PUBLIC '- //SAP//UWL1.0//EN' 'uwl_configuration.dtd'>
<UWLConfiguration version="1.0">
  <ItemTypes>
    <ItemType name="uwl.task.webflow.decision.TS00008267"
     connector="WebFlowConnector" defaultView="DefaultView"
     defaultAction="launchiViewAction" executionMode="default">
      <ItemTypeCriteria systemId="WFD" externalType="TS00008267"
       connector="WebFlowConnector"/>
      <Actions>
        <Action name="launchiViewAction" handler="IViewLauncher"
         launchInNewWindow ="yes">
          <Properties>
            <Property name="iview"
              value="pcd:portal_content/UWL_Book/Decision_Dashboard"/>
          </Properties>
          <Descriptions default=""/>
        </Action>
      </Actions>
    </ItemType>
  </ItemTypes>
</UWLConfiguration>
```

Listing 2.5 XML Configuration to Launch Portal Page

iView/page launching is also an option that you can configure in the back end SAP Business Workflow system, using transaction SWFVISU. You need to do this in two parts:

1. First, select the **Task Visualization** element, and create a new entry, entering the task type code and selecting the type **iView** for the **Visualization Type**, as shown in Figure 2.35.

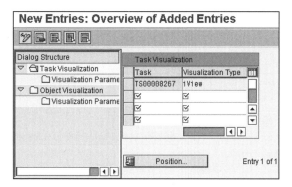

Figure 2.35 Creating a Task Entry in transaction SWFVISU

2. Next, you need to define the iView to be called. Select the subelement **Visualization Parameter**, select the table entry for the task you just created, and then right-click and select the option **Choose Subdialog**. This opens a screen like the one shown in Figure 2.36, where you should create an entry with the parameter set to **ID** and the value set to the PCD URL of the iView to launch for that task type.

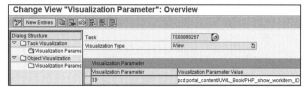

Figure 2.36 Define the iView for this Task Entry

3. After making the settings in transaction SWFVISU, you need to re-register this system for UWL (see "Registering Item Types" in Section 2.1).

Web Dynpro Applications

One of the more useful (and yet complex) ways of customizing UWL is to launch Web Dynpro applications to handle work items because it is very easy to produce professional-looking user-friendly web-enabled transactions in Web Dynpro. Right now, we'll focus on Web Dynpro

Java[18], but the principles are the same for Web Dynpro ABAP.

Just like for launching an iView (as you saw in "Portal iViews and Pages" in Section 2.4), transaction SWFVISU in the SAP Business Workflow back end can also be used to get UWL to launch a Web Dynpro. Instead of choosing **Visualization type iView**, choose **Java WebDynpro**; and instead of setting the **ID** parameter to the PCD URL, set the parameters shown in Table 2.5.

Parameter	Description
PACKAGE	Set this to the namespace and project.
APPLICATION	Set this to the application name within the project.
SYSTEM_ALIAS	The alias of the portal system landscape entry describes the system that the Web Dynpro is deployed to. The alias SAP_LocalSystem refers to the portal where UWL is running.

Table 2.5 SWFVISU Settings for Web Dynpro Applications

You can see this in action in the pair of screens shown in Figure 2.37 and Figure 2.38. The example shows a local Web Dynpro project **UWLbook** with an application **ShowWorkitemId,** which is deployed to run on the portal. The corresponding SWFVISU parameter values are listed here:

▶ APPLICATION: ShowWorkitemId
▶ PACKAGE: local/UWLbook
▶ SYSTEM_ALIAS: SAP_LocalSystem

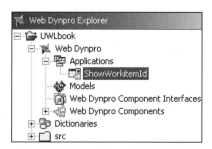

Figure 2.37 A Sample Web Dynpro Project in the SAP NetWeaver Development Studio

---

18 Here we look only at how to launch a Web Dynpro application. Section 3.2 shows how to construct a Web Dynpro application that will work with UWL and SAP Business Workflow.

```
<ItemType name="uwl.task.webflow.TS00008267" connector="WebFlowConnector"
 defaultView="DefaultView" defaultAction="launchWebDynPro"
 executionMode="default">
  <ItemTypeCriteria externalType="TS00008267" connector="WebFlowConnector"/>
  <Actions>
    <Action name="launchWebDynPro" handler="SAPWebDynproLauncher">
      <Properties>
        <Property name="WebDynproApplication" value="ShowWorkitemId"/>
        <Property name="WebDynproDeployableObject" value="local/UWLbook"/>
        <Property name="System" value="SAP_LocalSystem"/>
      </Properties>
    </Action>
  </Actions>
</ItemType>
```

Listing 2.6 XML Configuration for Launching a Web Dynpro Application

Task	TS00008267
Visualization Type	Java WebDynpro
Visualization Parameter	
Visualization Parameter	Visualization Parar
APPLICATION	ShowWorkitemId
PACKAGE	local/UWLbook
SYSTEM_ALIAS	SAP_LocalSystem

Figure 2.38 SWFVISU Settings for a Web Dynpro Project

Of course, there is also an XML configuration equivalent for this, shown in Listing 2.6.

The property names are changed a little in the XML file, so that APPLICATION becomes WebDynproApplication, PACKAGE becomes WebDynproDeployableObject, and SYSTEM_ALIAS becomes System.

Web Dynpro work item handlers will be shown in more detail in Section 3.3.1, and in Section 6.2, you'll see how to use Web Dynpro to build a work item handler for a BlackBerry handheld device.

2.5 Summary

This chapter has shown you how to connect your portal to a SAP Business Workflow system with UWL. You've seen how easy it is to customize some of the look-and-feel options, removing any buttons or columns that might otherwise distract your users. You've also learned how to get UWL to launch the GUI, URL, iView, or Web Dynpro of your choice when a user clicks on a work item. In other words, if you came in knowing nothing about setting up UWL, you now know most of what you need to use on most projects, and you also have the foundation skills necessary to tackle the rest of the book.

3 Customizing the Universal Worklist

In the previous chapter, you saw how to set up UWL, how to determine the layout of the UWL iView, and how to control what happens when a user clicks on a work item. In this chapter, the customization concept is taken further, and, among other things, you will see how to add custom attributes to the display (see Section 3.1), how to produce UWL views specific to certain types of tasks, and how to add decision buttons to the items in the list (see Section 3.2). You'll also learn how to create Web Dynpro Java applications (see Section 3.3) or custom portal components to process work items.

In the rest of this chapter, we'll use the workflow example of requesting and approving a leave of absence — you can find out how to set up that workflow in the SAP Help Portal at **Embedded Processes (SAP Business Workflow) • Reference • SAP Business Workflow Examples • Demo Example: Processing a Notification of Absence • Preparation and Customizing**. If you want to see some more detail behind the configuration of that workflow, check out the SAP Help Portal at **Business Task Management • Reference • Tutorials • Business Workflow – Tutorials • Tutorial: Workflow Modeling**. In this case, an administrator (Bob Cratchit) will be asking for leave from his boss (Ebenezer Scrooge).

3.1 Custom Attributes and Views

In this section, on custom views, we will find out how to add more than just the standard workflow attributes to the display of work items. To start with, you'll see how to bring in information from the business context of the work item (in this case, information about a leave of absence that is to be approved) and how to add that to the information shown in the list view of UWL. Then you'll see how to extend that information to the item

details screen, giving the workflow agent all the information necessary to make a decision immediately.

If you are unfamiliar with configuring the SAP Business Workflow, then see Appendix A for details on how to set up the Leave of Absence workflow used as an example in this section.

Custom Attributes

As well as the standard attributes used for displaying work items (discussed in Chapter 2), you can create UWL attributes from three sources:

▸ The portal's User Management Engine (UME)
▸ The ABAP Business Object Repository (BOR)
▸ The workflow or alert container for the task being processed

One of the challenges in setting up custom attributes in UWL is simply finding where the list of allowed attributes is documented. To save you the time of hunting through the SAP documentation, here is where to look:

▸ **Standard attributes**
The standard list of attributes, which is available for use in any UWL work item, is as follows: `appContext`, `attachmentCount`, `completedDate`, `connectorId`, `createdDate`, `creatorId`, `description`, `dueDate`, `escalatedBy`, `executionUrl`, `expiryDate`, `externalId`, `externalObjectId`, `externalType`, `forwardedBy`, `forwardedDate`, `internalId`, `isEscalated`, `itemType`, `memoCount`, `parentItemId`, `priority`, `processDueDate`, `processor`, `status`, `subject`, `subprocessId`, `substitutedFor`, `systemId`, and `userId`.
They are described in more detail in the SAP Help Portal at **Business Task Management • Universal Worklist configuration • Advanced Configuration • Task Launch Configuration • Standard Item Attributes**.

▶ **UME attributes**

The list of UME attributes, which give you information about the user, is in the SAP Help Portal at **Java Development Manual • Reference • Appendix • UME Reference • Logical Attributes**.

▶ **BOR attributes**

If you already know the technical name of a business object (e.g., FORMABSENC for the notification of absence example used in this chapter, or BUS2121 for a SRM shopping cart), then you can run transaction SWO1 and enter the object name. The resulting screen will give you the attribute names under **Key fields** and **Attributes** (see Figure 3.1). To use them in UWL, you must remove the object name and capitalize the field name, so AbsenceForm.CostCenter will become COSTCENTER. If you don't know the name of the business object, you can find out by looking at the workflow container for the task.

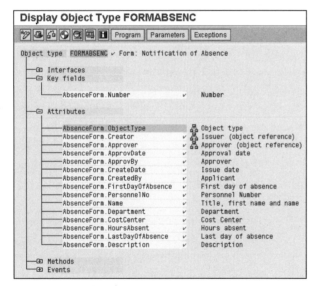

Figure 3.1 Using SWO1 to Examine BOR Attributes

▶ **Workflow container attributes**

Only top-level container attributes are available for the UWL, which can limit the usefulness of workflow container attributes. If you are using customized workflows, you should ask your workflow developer to make any necessary attributes available at the top level of the container.

The easiest way to discover the available container attributes is to use an existing work item ID and call

SAP_WAPI_READ_CONTAINER from transaction SE37. From the result screen, double-click on the SIMPLE_CONTAINER table result. As shown in Figure 3.2, the contents of the **ELEMENT** column are the container attributes you can use in your UWL configuration; the contents of the **VALUE** column are the corresponding values that will appear in UWL.

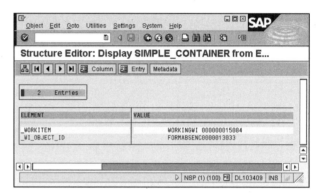

Figure 3.2 Container Attributes Shown by Calling SAP_WAPI_READ_CONTAINER

If you don't have an available work item, but you do know the task type, then you can run transaction PFTC_DIS to show task details. For our absence example, select **Standard task,** and enter task number "30000016". Select the **Container** tab, right-click, and select **Technical names on** to see the attribute names.

Wizard-Based Configuration

Now that you know how to find out the name of these attributes, the next step is to make them available for use on given task types:

1. For ABAP BOR attributes, go to the portal menu **System Administration • System Configuration • Universal Worklist & Workflow • Universal Worklist – Administration,** and click the link **Click to Configure Item Types and Customize Views Using a Wizard** (see Figure 3.3).

2. Select the option **Define custom attributes and customize the corresponding view,** and click the **Next** button.

3. In the next screen (see Figure 3.4), select the option **Create New Configuration,** enter a name for the new configuration (e.g., "Absence Form"), enter the Task ID (e.g., "TS3000016"), and click the **Next** button.

4. On the next screen, choose the back end system you want to customize, and then click **Next**. Now you can see, as shown in Figure 3.5, the list of available attributes for the business object. This screen also allows you to select the attributes you want to make available in UWL for work items of your chosen task type.

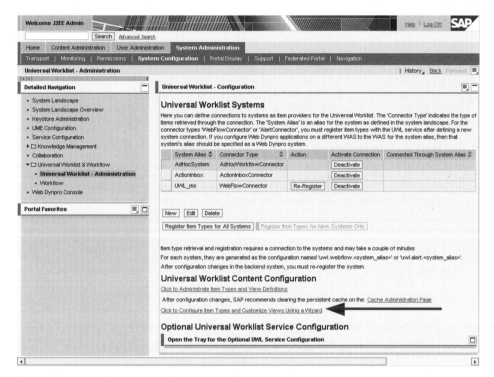

Figure 3.3 Link for Wizard-Based UWL Configuration

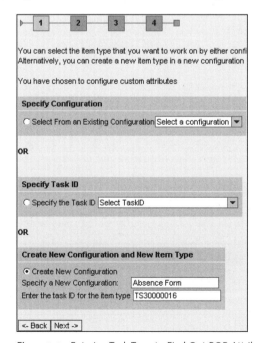

Figure 3.4 Entering Task Type to Find Out BOR Attributes

Figure 3.5 Attributes for Business Object FORMABSENC Retrieved from Task Type TS30000016

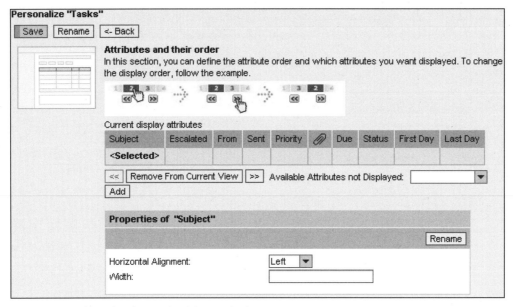

Figure 3.6   Set the Order of Normal and Custom Attributes

5. Check the boxes of the attributes you want to use and provide the name to show in UWL. For example, you might select the attributes FIRSTDAYOFABSENCE and LASTDAYOFABSENCE and give them the descriptions "First Day" and "Last Day", respectively. When you're done, click the **Next** button.

6. Now you will see the **Personalize Tasks** screen, similar to the screen that end users see. Make sure that the column order for the attributes is as you want it. Figure 3.6 shows the new attributes at the right-hand side. Click the **Save** button.

7. On the next screen, choose the option of applying this configuration to the relevant back end system or to all systems, and then click the **Apply to systems** button.

8. This will result in a new UWL configuration XML file customized.uwl.webflow.WFD, assuming the back end system alias is WFD.

Now, although this is a wizard-based configuration, you still need to do some postprocessing to use it properly:

1. You need to configure the UWL iView to use the XML file's View configuration. Look through the generated XML file to find the line beginning: <View name="uwl.task.webflow.TS30000016_view".

2. Edit the sap_uwl_viewname property of your UWL iView (see Chapter 2 for details) to be the same as this name.

3. Farther down in the <View> section of the XML file, you will need to add entries for your new attributes to the existing <DisplayAttribute> entries, as shown in Listing 3.1.

```
<DisplayAttribute name="FIRSTDAYOFABSENCE"
    type="date">
 <Descriptions default="First Day"/>
</DisplayAttribute>
<DisplayAttribute name="LASTDAYOFABSENCE"
    type="date">
 <Descriptions default="Last Day"/>
</DisplayAttribute>
```

Listing 3.1   Adding DisplayAttribute Entries to the Generated XML File

Tip

You need to clear the UWL caches to see the resulting changes from an XML configuration change (see Section 2.3 for more details on clearing the caches). If you add or remove a View definition, then users will have to log out and log in again to see the resulting change.

Direct XML Configuration

If you want to display UME-based or container-based custom attributes as well as ABAP BOR attributes, then you need to create an XML configuration file directly instead.

Custom Attributes: Not Just for Show

Custom attributes defined in XML configurations don't have to be displayed; you may just want them available for use as parameters in launch actions (see Section 2.4).

Listing 3.2 shows a sample XML configuration using custom attributes from all three sources: ABAP BOR, webflow container, and UME. In the `<CustomAttributes>` section of the listing, you can see three `<CustomAttributeSource>` elements with the `id` attributes set to `ABAP_BOR`, `WEBFLOW_CONTAINER`, and `UM`; these dictate the data source for the embedded `<Attribute>` elements. The following `<View>` section then defines how these attributes are shown as columns in the UWL.

```xml
<?xml version="1.0" encoding="utf-8"?>
<!DOCTYPE UWLConfiguration PUBLIC '-//SAP//UWL1.0//EN' 'uwl_configuration.dtd' []>
<UWLConfiguration version="1.0">
 <ItemTypes>
    <ItemType name="uwl.task.webflow.TS30000016" connector="WebFlowConnector"
        defaultView="myApprovalView" defaultAction="viewDetail"
        executionMode="pessimistic">
    <ItemTypeCriteria externalType="TS30000016" connector="WebFlowConnector"/>
    <CustomAttributes>
      <CustomAttributeSource id="ABAP_BOR" objectIdHolder="externalObjectId"
          objectType="FORMABSENC" cacheValidity="final">
        <Attribute name="LASTDAYOFABSENCE" type="date"
           displayName="Last day of absence"/>
        <Attribute name="FIRSTDAYOFABSENCE" type="date"
           displayName="First day of absence"/>
      </CustomAttributeSource>
      <CustomAttributeSource id="WEBFLOW_CONTAINER" objectIdHolder="externalId"
          objectType="WebFlowContainer" cacheValidity="default">
        <Attribute name="_WI_OBJECT_ID" type="string" displayName="_WI_OBJECT_ID"/>
      </CustomAttributeSource>
      <CustomAttributeSource id="UM" objectIdHolder="creatorId" objectType="user"
          cacheValidity="final">
        <Attribute name="firstName" type="string" displayName="firstName"/>
        <Attribute name="lastName" type="string" displayName="lastName"/>
      </CustomAttributeSource>
    </CustomAttributes>
    </ItemType>
 </ItemTypes>
<Views>
    <View name="myApprovalView" width="98%"
```

Listing 3.2   Sample XML File to Display Custom Attributes

```
           supportedItemTypes="uwl.task.webflow.TS30000016"
           columnOrder="attachmentCount, detailIcon, subject, createdDate, firstName,
              lastName, FIRSTDAYOFABSENCE, LASTDAYOFABSENCE, _WI_OBJECT_ID"
           sortby="createdDate" visibleRowCount="10" headerVisible="yes"
           selectionMode="SINGLESELECT" tableDesign="STANDARD"
           tableNavigationFooterVisible="yes" emphasizedItems="new"
           displayOnlyDefinedAttributes="no">
        <Descriptions default="Vacation Requests to Approve">
          <ShortDescriptions>
            <Description Language="en" Description="Vacation Requests to Approve"/>
          </ShortDescriptions>
        </Descriptions>
        <DisplayAttributes>
          <DisplayAttribute name="FIRSTDAYOFABSENCE" type="date" width=""
              sortable="yes" format="medium">
            <Descriptions default="Vacation begins on"/>
          </DisplayAttribute>
          <DisplayAttribute name="LASTDAYOFABSENCE" type="date" width=""
              sortable="yes" format="medium">
            <Descriptions default="Vacation Ends On"/>
          </DisplayAttribute>
          <DisplayAttribute name="_WI_OBJECT_ID" type="string" width="" sortable="yes"
              format="medium" />
          <DisplayAttribute name="firstName" type="string" width="" sortable="yes"
              format="medium" />
          <DisplayAttribute name="lastName" type="string" width="" sortable="yes"
              format="medium" />
        </DisplayAttributes>
      </View>
    </Views>
</UWLConfiguration>
```

Listing 3.2 Sample XML File to Display Custom Attributes (cont.)

You can see the effects of this configuration in Figure 3.7: The originator of the work items, the SAP Business Workflow system user WF-BATCH, has been mapped to the portal and given a first name of "SAP" and a last name of "Workflow System" to highlight the UME attributes.

Note that for each attribute that is made available in a CustomAttributeSource element, that attribute is dis-

played onscreen as a result of the columnOrder attribute of the View element and the existence of a corresponding DisplayAttribute element. Setting the defaultView attribute of an ItemType element to the name of a custom-defined view leads to the standard UWL display giving users the option of choosing that view if there are any appropriate items in the list (see Figure 3.8).

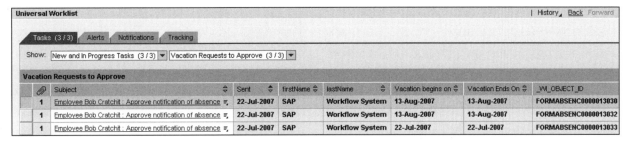

Figure 3.7   Result of Applying the XML Configuration from Listing 3.2

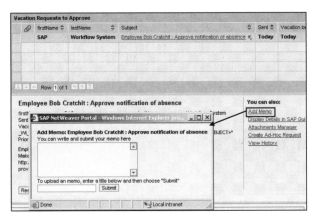

Figure 3.8   Subview Menu Gives Access to Custom View

Adding Notes

Although not enabled by default, you can give users the ability to add a comment or note to a work item in their worklists (see Figure 3.9). To do this, just add the following line to the `Actions` section of the relevant task's `ItemType` element in the XML configuration:

```
<Action reference="addMemo"/>
```

You can even make this apply to all work items by adding the line to the generic task `uwl.task.webflow`. For decision-based work items, you can use the User Decision action handler (see "User Decision Handler" in Section 3.2) to control whether or not a user must enter a note to proceed with a given decision.

3.2   Alternative Action Handlers

Now that you have a custom view for just the tasks of a certain type, you can add buttons for user decisions and give users the option of adding comments for their decisions. There are four kinds of action handlers that are useful here (see Section 2.4 for a complete list of action handlers):

▶ User Decision handler

▶ Terminating Event handler

▶ Updating Container handler

▶ Function Module handler

A brief description of each handler is given in this section, with working examples (shown as differences from Listing 3.2). More complete documentation can be found in the SAP Help Portal in the **UWL API Documentation for Action Handlers** (see Table B.2 in Appendix B for the link).

User Decision Handler

> **A Note on Decision Tasks**
>
> In terms of the demo workflow we are using, the absence approve/reject step is not a true decision step in the workflow sense; instead, it relies on the events following on from updating the `FORMABSENC` business object. For the User Decision handler, a true decision step needs to be used (one for which the function module `SAP_WAPI_DECISION_READ` returns alternatives), such as task type `TS00008267`, as used in the examples from Section 2.4.

Figure 3.9   Add Memo Link and Resulting Pop-Up

The User Decision handler looks up the descriptions of the decision options in the back end system and shows them to the user as decision buttons in the item detail area (see Figure 3.10).

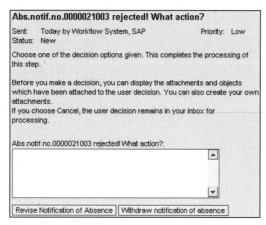

Figure 3.10 User Decision Handler with Note

Listing 3.3 shows the XML configuration for the User Decision handler. Points to note are the addition of `.decision.` to the item type name, which signals UWL to read the text for the decision keys from the back end sys-tem; and the property `UserDecisionNote` set to `manda-tory` for one of the choices. This means that if users make that choice, then they must enter some text to explain their decision. The usual case for this is to explain a rejection, but in this case, the note is necessary for the employees to explain why they are resubmitting an already-rejected leave request.

Terminating Event Handler

The Terminating Event handler creates a workflow event on the specified business object. It is configured by adding `Action` elements to the `ItemType`'s `Actions` tag as shown in Listing 3.4.

Note

Although this example shows events being raised on the absence approval object, this is not enough in itself to approve or reject an absence in the SAP absence approval demo workflow because terminating event handlers are not implemented as standard on task TS30000016.

```
<ItemType
    name="uwl.task.webflow.decision.TS00008267"
    connector="WebFlowConnector"
    defaultView="DefaultView">
  <ItemTypeCriteria externalType="TS00008267" connector="WebFlowConnector"/>
  <Actions>
    <Action name="withdraw" groupAction="yes" handler="UserDecisionHandler">
      <Properties>
        <Property name="decisionKey" value="2"/>
      </Properties>
    </Action>
    <Action name="revise" groupAction="yes" handler="UserDecisionHandler">
      <Properties>
        <Property name="decisionKey" value="1"/>
        <Property name="UserDecisionNote" value="mandatory"/>
      </Properties>
    </Action>
  </Actions>
</ItemType>
```

Listing 3.3 XML Configuration for User Decision Handler with Mandatory Note

```
...
<!-- Added to the ItemType's Actions tag -->
<Action name="approved" groupAction="yes" handler="TerminatingEventHandler">
  <Properties>
    <Property name="objectType" value="FORMABSENC"/>
    <Property name="eventName" value="approved"/>
    <Property name="objectId" value="${item.externalObjectId}"/>
  </Properties>
  <Descriptions default="Approve"/>
</Action>
<Action name="rejected" groupAction="yes" handler="TerminatingEventHandler">
  <Properties>
    <Property name="objectType" value="FORMABSENC"/>
    <Property name="eventName" value="rejected"/>
    <Property name="objectId" value="${item.externalObjectId}"/>
  </Properties>
  <Descriptions default="Reject"/>
</Action>
...
```

Listing 3.4   XML Modifications for TerminatingEventHandler Decision Buttons

Updating Container Handler

The Updating Container handler updates elements of the workflow container with the specified values. For the absence approval example, you must set the _WI_RESULT and _RESULT elements of the container to R for Reject and A for Approve. The configuration for this is shown in Listing 3.5.

Note

Although this example shows the container being updated for task TS30000016, this is not enough in itself to approve or reject an absence in the SAP absence approval demo workflow because the FORM-ABSENC object must also be updated.

Function Module Action Handler

The Function Module action handler calls a configurable function module by RFC in the SAP Business Workflow system. You can specify import parameters for the function module using Property elements in the XML and

setting the name and value attributes of the element to the name and value of the import parameter. You can specify table data for import as a series of Property tags as follows:

▶ The first table you specify has the property name UWL_TABLE_IN1 with the value set to the actual table name, for example:
```
<Property name="UWL_TABLE_IN1"
          value="PEOPLE_TAB"/>
```

▶ Each field in each row of the table then requires two Property tags: one for the field name and one for the field value, for example:
```
<Property name="UWL_TABLE_IN1_ROW1_
  PARAMETER1" value="FIRST_NAME"/>
<Property name="UWL_TABLE_IN1_ROW1_
  PARAMETER1_VALUE" value="BOB"/>
```

▶ The other fields in each row have similar property names, but ..._PARAMETER1... becomes ..._PARAMETER2..., ..._PARAMETER3, and so on. Similarly, subsequent rows are ..._ROW1_..., ..._ROW2_..., and so on, and any other tables are

```
...
<!-- Added to the ItemType's Actions tag -->
      <Action name="approved" userDecision="yes" handler="UpdatingContainerHandler">
        <Properties>
          <Property name="_WI_RESULT" value="A"/>
          <Property name="_RESULT" value="A"/>
        </Properties>
        <Descriptions default="Approve"/>
      </Action>
      <Action name="rejected" userDecision="yes" handler="UpdatingContainerHandler">
        <Properties>
          <Property name="_WI_RESULT" value="R"/>
          <Property name="_RESULT" value="R"/>
        </Properties>
        <Descriptions default="Reject"/>
      </Action>
...
```

Listing 3.5 XML Modifications for UpdatingContainerHandler Decision Buttons

named UWL_TABLE_IN2, UWL_TABLE_IN3, and so on. You can see this in more detail in Listing 3.6.

At the time of writing (using SAP NetWeaver 7.0 SPS09), the example in Listing 3.6 caused an extra, empty row to be added to the INPUT_CONTAINER table, which resulted in an error when calling SAP_WAPI_CREATE_EVENT. SAP may have fixed this bug by the time you read this.

```
...
<!-- Added to the ItemType's Actions tag -->
<Action name="approved" groupAction="yes" handler="FunctionModuleActionHandler">
  <Properties>
    <Property name="FunctionModule" value="SAP_WAPI_CREATE_EVENT"/>
    <Property name="OBJECT_TYPE" value="FORMABSENC"/>
    <Property name="EVENT" value="approved"/>
    <Property name="OBJECT_KEY" value="${item.externalObjectId}"/>
    <Property name="COMMIT_WORK" value="X"/>
    <!-- special return parameters -->
    <Property name="UWL_RETURN_CODE" value="RET_MESS"/>
    <!-- special input parameters -->
    <Property name="UWL_TABLE_IN1" value="INPUT_CONTAINER"/>
    <Property name="UWL_TABLE_IN1_ROW1_PARAMETER1" value="ELEMENT"/>
```

Listing 3.6 XML Modifications for FunctionModuleActionHandler Decision Buttons

```
    <Property name="UWL_TABLE_IN1_ROW1_PARAMETER1_VALUE" value="_WI_RESULT"/>
    <Property name="UWL_TABLE_IN1_ROW1_PARAMETER2" value="VALUE"/>
    <Property name="UWL_TABLE_IN1_ROW1_PARAMETER2_VALUE" value="A"/>
    <Property name="UWL_TABLE_IN1_ROW2_PARAMETER1" value="ELEMENT"/>
    <Property name="UWL_TABLE_IN1_ROW2_PARAMETER1_VALUE" value="_RESULT"/>
    <Property name="UWL_TABLE_IN1_ROW2_PARAMETER2" value="VALUE"/>
    <Property name="UWL_TABLE_IN1_ROW2_PARAMETER2_VALUE" value="A"/>
  </Properties>
  <Descriptions default="Approve"/>
</Action>
<Action name="rejected" groupAction="yes" handler="FunctionModuleActionHandler">
  <Properties>
    <Property name="FunctionModule" value="SAP_WAPI_CREATE_EVENT"/>
    <Property name="OBJECT_TYPE" value="FORMABSENC"/>
    <Property name="EVENT" value="rejected"/>
    <Property name="OBJECT_KEY" value="${item.externalObjectId}"/>
    <Property name="COMMIT_WORK" value="X"/>
    <Property name="UWL_RETURN_CODE" value="RET_MESS"/>
    <Property name="UWL_TABLE_IN1" value="INPUT_CONTAINER"/>
    <Property name="UWL_TABLE_IN1_ROW1_PARAMETER1" value="ELEMENT"/>
    <Property name="UWL_TABLE_IN1_ROW1_PARAMETER1_VALUE" value="_WI_RESULT"/>
    <Property name="UWL_TABLE_IN1_ROW1_PARAMETER2" value="VALUE"/>
    <Property name="UWL_TABLE_IN1_ROW1_PARAMETER2_VALUE" value="R"/>
    <Property name="UWL_TABLE_IN1_ROW2_PARAMETER1" value="ELEMENT"/>
    <Property name="UWL_TABLE_IN1_ROW2_PARAMETER1_VALUE" value="_RESULT"/>
    <Property name="UWL_TABLE_IN1_ROW2_PARAMETER2" value="VALUE"/>
    <Property name="UWL_TABLE_IN1_ROW2_PARAMETER2_VALUE" value="R"/>
  </Properties>
  <Descriptions default="Reject"/>
...
```

Listing 3.6   XML Modifications for FunctionModuleActionHandler Decision Buttons (cont.)

Note

Although this example shows SAP_WAPI_CREATE_ EVENT being called, this is not enough in itself to approve or reject an absence in the SAP absence approval demo workflow because terminating event handlers are not implemented as standard on task TS30000016.

Making Decisions in Bulk

You can give your users the ability to make several decisions at once about a set of similar items in their worklist by creating a custom view with radio buttons for making the decision. You can see the configuration for this in Listing 3.7. Just add two DisplayAttribute elements, which refer via actionRef attributes to existing actions, and add the names of these new attributes to the columnOrder attribute of the View.

```
<!-- Add columns to the View's columnOrder attribute -->
<View name="myApprovalView" supportedItemTypes="uwl.task.webflow.TS30000016"
   columnOrder="attachmentCount, detailIcon, subject, createdDate,
   FIRSTDAYOFABSENCE, LASTDAYOFABSENCE, rejectCol, approveCol">
...
<!-- Added to the View's DisplayAttributes tag -->
<DisplayAttribute name="rejectCol" type="radiobutton" width="" actionRef="rejected">
  <Descriptions default="Reject">
  </Descriptions>
</DisplayAttribute>
<DisplayAttribute name="approveCol" type="radiobutton" width="" actionRef="approved">
  <Descriptions default="Approve">
  </Descriptions>
</DisplayAttribute>
...
<!-- Added to the View's Actions tag -->
<Action reference="submitUserDecisions" />
...
```

Listing 3.7 Adding Decision Options to the List View

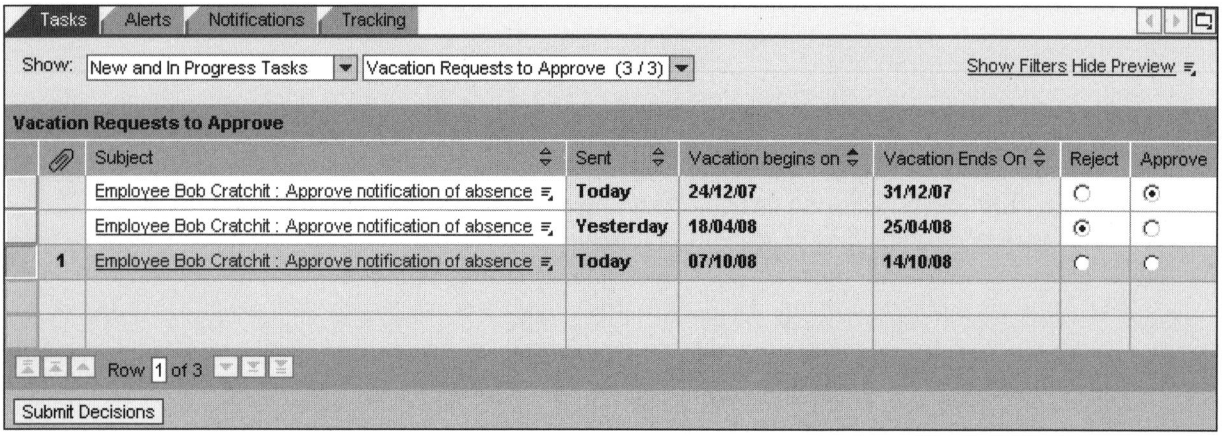

Figure 3.11 Making Several Decisions at Once

You can see the result of this configuration in Figure 3.11. The approver just selects the radio button entry for each decision and then clicks the **Submit Decisions** button. The defined action handler is called for each entry that has a selected decision (so none would be called for the third entry in the figure because neither radio button is selected).

3.3   Custom Work Item Handlers

In the previous sections, you saw how to configure UWL with SAP-standard content. In the workshops in this section, you will learn how to build Web Dynpro and HTMLB for Java applications, which will be run when a user clicks on an item in UWL.

Workshop 1: Web Dynpro Application Item Handler

This is not the place to go into detail about how to create and deploy a Web Dynpro Java application; there are other SAP PRESS books that do a better job of that.[1] For the purposes of this exercise, we will assume that you know how to build a Web Dynpro Java application, and we'll just cover the elements specific to our scenario.

For the notification of absence example, the application needs to get the details of a task type TS30000016 work item and then ask the approver to make a decision before registering that decision with the SAP Business Workflow system. The steps to do this are described next.

Definition of the Sample Application

The approval application has three screens, as shown in the upper part of the data model diagram in Figure 3.12.

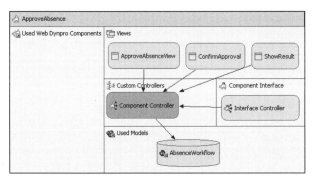

Figure 3.12 Data Model for the Application

▶ The first screen shows the details of the absence. If the absence has not yet been approved, there will be **Approve** and **Reject** buttons; otherwise, the user will be told that the item has already been processed.

▶ When the approver clicks a button, the next screen asks them to confirm the decision ("Are you sure? Yes/No."). If the approver answers **No**, the approver is taken back to the first screen; if the approver answers **Yes**, the decision is processed in the SAP Business Workflow system.

▶ Having confirmed the decision, the third screen informs the user that the decision has been processed by SAP Business Workflow.

Initial Work Item Display

Before there is any interaction with the user, the Web Dynpro application needs to find out the work item ID from the HTTP request, use that to call functions in SAP Business Workflow to get the work item details, and then display those details to the user. This is a slightly complex process (shown diagrammatically in Figure 3.13):

1. The onPlugDefault plug of the Interface View is configured to accept a parameter wi_id of type string. This is where the HTTP request parameter wi_id from the UWL link is passed into the application.

2. The onPlugDefault() method of the Interface View calls a method on the Interface Controller, which in turn sets the value of the work item ID as a context attribute of the Component Controller and then passes control to the Component Controller by calling its getItemDetails() method.

3. The getItemDetails() method of the Component Controller calls into the SAP Business Workflow system via the Web Dynpro Model layer to get information about the work item.

4. getItemDetails() then sets the values of the view elements to reflect the work item information.

5. Control passes back to the Interface View, which renders the Web Dynpro page to the user's browser with all the information filled in.

Web Dynpro applications are built using the Model-View-Controller philosophy: business data is provided by the Model (calls to function modules in our case); the View is created in the Web Dynpro Visual Designer by dragging and dropping user interface elements onto a form; and the Controller contains the Java code and Web Dynpro configuration that determine the application flow. These elements of the application are built according to the following sections.

Building the Navigation

The first thing to do in creating the Web Dynpro action handler is to create a project in the SAP NetWeaver Developer Studio and then set up the pages and the basic navigation framework for them (part of the view), as shown in the following steps:

1. Create a Web Dynpro project, and make sure it has access to the component com.sap.security.api,

---

1 For example, *Mastering SAP Enterprise Portal 6.0 Application Development* (SAP PRESS Essentials, 2006) describes in good detail how to build and deploy a Web Dynpro application.

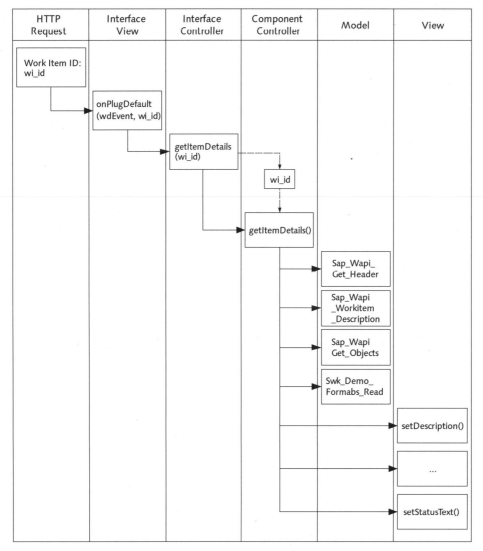

Figure 3.13   Sequence Diagram for Initial Display of Work Item

either as a DC (Development Component) if you created a NWDI (SAP NetWeaver Development Infrastructure) development component, or by finding
com.sap.security.api.jar and adding it to the *lib*
directory of your project, if you created a local project.
Make sure the library is on the project build path.

2. Create three views: ApproveAbsenceView (the default
view), ConfirmApproval, and ShowResult.

3. Create navigation links between the views as in Table
3.1. The result should look like Figure 3.14.

Source View	Source Plug	Destination View	Destina-tion Plug
Approve-AbsenceView	toCon-firma-tion	Confirm-Approval	from-Approval
Confirm-Approval	toAp-proval	ApproveAb-senceView	fromCon-firmation
Confirm-Approval	toResult	ShowResult	fromCon-firmation

Table 3.1   Navigation Links

Figure 3.14   Navigation Flow for Absence Approval

4. Add the Interface Controller as a required controller of the Interface View, and then add the body of the `onPlugDefault()` method as shown in Listing 3.8.

```
public void onPlugDefault(
  IWDCustomEvent wdEvent,
  String wi_id)
{
  //@@begin onPlugDefault(ServerEvent)
  wdThis.wdGetApproveAbsenceInterface
    Controller()
    .getItemDetails(wi_id);
  //@@end
}
```

Listing 3.8   Interface View onPlugDefault() Method

5. Add the `getItemDetails()` method to the Interface Controller, taking a parameter `wi_id` of type `String`. Add the body of this method as shown in Listing 3.9.

```
public void getItemDetails(String wi_id)
{
  //@@begin getItemDetails()
  wdContext.currentContextElement()
    .setWi_id(wi_id);
  wdThis.wdGetApproveAbsenceController()
    .getItemDetails();
  //@@end
}
```

Listing 3.9   Interface Controller getItemDetails() Method

Creating the Model

Now that the basic application structure is in place, it's time to flesh it out, starting with the Web Dynpro Model layer, that is, the access layer for the function modules in the SAP Business Workflow system.

1. Create an adaptive RFC model containing the following function modules:
   - ▶ SAP_WAPI_GET_WORKITEM_DETAIL
   - ▶ SAP_WAPI_GET_OBJECTS
   - ▶ SAP_WAPI_WORKITEM_DESCRIPTION
   - ▶ SWK_DEMO_FORMABS_READ
   - ▶ SWK_DEMO_FORMABS_PROC_WRITE
   - ▶ SAP_WAPI_WORKITEM_COMPLETE

2. Map the context elements from the Model Context to the Component Context as shown in Table 3.2 to Table 3.7.

Component Context	Model Context
User	User
Workitem_Id	Workitem_Id
detailOutput • Workitem_ Detail • Note_Count	Output • Workitem_Detail • Note_Count
detailOutput • Workitem_ Detail • Wi_Stat	Output • Workitem_Detail • Wi_Stat
detailOutput • Workitem_ Detail • Wi_Text	Output • Workitem_Detail • Wi_Text
detailOutput • detailMessage_Lines • Line	Output • Message_Lines • Line
detailOutput • detailMessage_Lines • Msg_type	Output • Message_Lines • Msg_type

Table 3.2   Context Mapping for SAP_WAPI_GET_WORKITEM_DETAIL_INPUT

Component Context	Model Context
User	User
Workitem_Id	Workitem_Id
objectOutput • Leading_ Object_2 • Instid	Output • Leading_Object_2 • Instid
objectOutput • Leading_ Object_2 • Typeid	Output • Leading_Object_2 • Typeid
objectOutput • objectMessage_Lines • Line	Output • Message_Lines • Line
objectOutput • objectMessage_Lines • Msg_type	Output • Message_Lines • Msg_type

Table 3.3   Context Mapping for SAP_WAPI_GET_OBJECTS_INPUT

Component Context	Model Context
User	User
Workitem_Id	Workitem_Id
descriptionOutput • Text_Lines • Textline	Output • Text_Lines • Textline

Table 3.4   Context Mapping for SAP_WAPI_WORKITEM_DESCRIPTION_INPUT

Component Context	Model Context
descriptionOutput • detailMessage_Lines • Line	Output • Message_Lines • Line
descriptionOutput • detailMessage _Lines • Msg_type	Output • Message_Lines • Msg_type

Table 3.4 Context Mapping for SAP_WAPI_WORKITEM_ DESCRIPTION_INPUT (cont.)

Component Context	Model Context
Im_Formnumber	Im_Formnumber
formreadOutput • E_Formdata • Abshours1	Output • E_Formdata • Abshours1
formreadOutput • E_Formdata • Abshours2	Output • E_Formdata • Abshours2
formreadOutput • E_Formdata • Abshours3	Output • E_Formdata • Abshours3
formreadOutput • E_Formdata • Firstday1	Output • E_Formdata • Firstday1
formreadOutput • E_Formdata • Firstday2	Output • E_Formdata • Firstday2
formreadOutput • E_Formdata • Firstday3	Output • E_Formdata • Firstday3
formreadOutput • E_Formdata • Lastday1	Output • E_Formdata • Lastday1
formreadOutput • E_Formdata • Lastday2	Output • E_Formdata • Lastday2
formreadOutput • E_Formdata • Lastday3	Output • E_Formdata • Lastday3
formreadOutput • E_Formdata • Reason	Output • E_Formdata • Reason

Table 3.5 Context Mapping for SWK_DEMO_FORMABS_READ

Component Context	Model Context
Im_Approvby	Im_Approvby
Im_Approvdate	Im_Approvdate
Im_Formnumber	Im_Formnumber
Im_Procstate	Im_Procstate
formOutput • E_Message	Output • E_Message
formOutput • E_Retcode	Output • E_ Retcode

Table 3.6 Context Mapping for SWK_DEMO_FORMABS_PROC_ WRITE_INPUT

Component Context	Model Context
Actual_Agent	Actual_Agent
Workitem_Id	Workitem_Id
completeOutput • completeMessage_Lines • Line	Output • Message_Lines • Line
completeOutput • complete-Message _Lines • Msg_type	Output • Message_Lines • Msg_type

Table 3.7 Context Mapping for SAP_WAPI_WORKITEM_ COMPLETE_INPUT

Component Controller – Initial View Population

With the model in place, the next job is to build the user interface for each screen (the main part of the view).

1. Create context value attributes on the Component Controller for the following values of type `string`:
   - `wi_id`
   - `user_id`
   - `form_id`
   - `approve_reject_flag`
   - `description`
   - `statusText`
   - `leave1`
   - `leave2`
   - `leave3`
   - `reason`

2. Create context value attributes on the Component Controller for the following values of type `com.sap.ide.webdynpro.uielementdefinitions. Visibility`:
   - `leave1_visibility`
   - `leave2_visibility`
   - `leave3_visibility`
   - `buttonVisibility`

3. Implement the Component Controller method `getItemDetails()` (see Listing 3.10) and its helper methods (Listing 3.11 has just the comments for these methods; see Appendix C for the full listing). This is the method that gets all of the information together for the work item to show to the user on the first screen.

```
public void getItemDetails( )
{
  //@@begin getItemDetails()
  logger.entering();
  manager = wdComponentAPI.getMessageManager();
  StringBuffer bufStatus = new StringBuffer();

  String workitem_id = wdContext.currentContextElement().getWi_id();
  if (workitem_id == null)
  {
    wdContext.currentContextElement().setStatusText("Error: no wi_id parameter.");
    return;
  }
  // Get the work item detail & description from SAP Business Workflow
  getWorkitemDetail(workitem_id);
  String description = getWorkitemDescription(workitem_id);

  // Get the form ID
  String formId = getFormId(workitem_id);
  wdContext.currentContextElement().setForm_id(formId);

  // Get the form details and set the context values for leave[1-3] and reason
  getFormDetails(formId);

  // If the work item is already completed,
  //   don't show the approve & reject buttons
  if (STATUS_COMPLETED.equals(
    wdContext.currentWorkitem_DetailElement().getWi_Stat()))
  {
    bufStatus.append("This item has already been processed.\n");
    wdContext.currentContextElement().setButtonVisibility(WDVisibility.NONE);
  }
  else
  {
    wdContext.currentContextElement().setButtonVisibility(WDVisibility.VISIBLE);
  }

  // Add a warning if there are any attachments to the work item
  if (this.numAttachments > 0)
  {
```

Listing 3.10   getItemDetails() Method of the Component Controller

```
    bufStatus.append("This item has attachments \
      - these cannot be viewed on a BlackBerry.\n");
  }


  wdContext.currentContextElement().setDescription(description);
  wdContext.currentContextElement().setStatusText(bufStatus.toString());


  logger.exiting();
  //@@end
}
```

Listing 3.10   getItemDetails() Method of the Component Controller (cont.)

```
private void getWorkitemDetail(String workitem_id)
{
     // Call SAP_WAPI_GET_WORKITEM_DETAIL with workitem_id as input

     // Retrieve note_count and wi_stat from the RFC call output
}


private String getFormId(String workitem_id)
{
     // Call SAP_WAPI_GET_OBJECTS with workitem_id as input

     // Retrieve Typeid and Instid from the RFC output, as formType and formNumber

     // If the form type is an absence form, return the form number.
     // Otherwise, report an error.
}

private String getWorkitemDescription(String workitem_id)
{
     // Call SAP_WAPI_WORKITEM_DESCRIPTION with workitem_id as input

     // Build up a description line by line from the RFC Text_Lines table

     // Return the description as a string
}


private void getFormDetails(String form_id)
{
```

Listing 3.11   Helper Methods for getItemDetails() (Comments Only)

```
        // Call SWK_DEMO_FORMABS_READ with form_id as input

        // Build up description of the first leave entry from RFC output values
        //   Firstday1, Lastday1, and Abshours1

        // Build up description of the second leave entry from RFC output values
        //   Firstday2, Lastday2, and Abshours2

        // Build up description of the third leave entry from RFC output values
        //   Firstday3, Lastday3, and Abshours3

        // Set the leave and visibility context attributes
        //   according to whether each start date is null or not
}
```

Listing 3.11   Helper Methods for getItemDetails() (Comments Only) (cont.)

4. Map the following context elements from the Component Controller to `ApproveAbsenceView`:
   - `detailOutput • Workitem_Detail • Wi_Text`
   - `description`
   - `leave1`
   - `leave1_visibility`
   - `leave2`
   - `leave2_visibility`
   - `leave3`
   - `leave3_visibility`
   - `formreadOutput • E_Formdata • Reason`
   - `statusText`
   - `approve_reject_flag`
   - `buttonVisibility`

5. Add elements to the `ApproveAbsenceView` view (see Table 3.8, Figure 3.15, and Figure 3.16):

View Element	Comments
RootUIElementContainer	Set the layout property to GridLayout.
HeadingTextView	Bind the text property to the Wi_Text context element, and set the design property to emphasized.
DescriptionTextView	Bind the text property to the description context element.

Table 3.8   Elements of the ApprovalAbsenceView View

View Element	Comments
Leave1TextView	Bind the text property to the leave1 context element and the visible property to the leave1_visibility element.
Leave2TextView	Bind the text property to the leave2 context element and the visible property to the leave2_visibility element.
Leave3TextView	Bind the text property to the leave3 context element and the visible property to the leave3_visibility element.
ReasonTextView	Bind the text property to the Reason context element.
ButtonContainer	This TransparentContainer element contains the Approve-Button and RejectButton.
ApproveButton	Set the text property to Approve and the visible property to the buttonVisibility context element.
RejectButton	Set the text property to Reject and the visible property to the buttonVisibility context element.
StatusTextView	Bind the text property to the statusText context element.

Table 3.8   Elements of the ApprovalAbsenceView View (cont.)

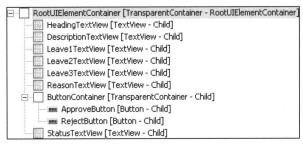

Figure 3.15 ApprovalAbsenceView Element Structure

Figure 3.16 ApprovalAbsenceView in the View Designer

6. At this stage, other than creating the application (see step 1 in "Preparing the Final View and Creating the Application" later in this chapter), you have done enough to display the work item details. What follows is the remaining code and configuration to enable processing of the approver's decision.

7. For the **Approve** button's onAction property, create a new action ApproveClicked, which fires the toConfirmation plug.

8. For the **Reject** button's onAction property, create a new action RejectClicked, which fires the toConfirmation plug.

Component Controller — Confirm Decision
Now that the view part of the application is in place, you can fill in the rest of the controller code:

1. Modify the onActionApproveClicked method as shown in Listing 3.12. This method says that when a user clicks the **Approve** button, the application remembers the approval and then moves on to the confirmation screen.

```
public void onActionApproveClicked(
    IWDCustomEvent wdEvent )
{
  //@@begin onActionApproveClicked(
    ServerEvent)
  wdContext.currentContextElement()
        .setApprove_reject_flag(
```

```
          ApproveAbsence.APPROVED);
  wdThis.wdGetApproveAbsenceController()
        .createConfirmQuestion();
  wdThis.wdFirePlugToConfirmation();
  //@@end
}
```
Listing 3.12 Modified onActionApproveClicked() Method

2. Modify the onActionRejectClicked method as shown in Listing 3.13. This method says that when a user clicks the **Reject** button, the application remembers the rejection and then moves on to the confirmation screen.

```
public void onActionRejectClicked(
    IWDCustomEvent wdEvent )
{
  //@@begin onActionRejectClicked(
    ServerEvent)
  wdContext.currentContextElement()
        .setApprove_reject_flag(
            ApproveAbsence.REJECTED);
  wdThis.wdGetApproveAbsenceController()
        .createConfirmQuestion();
  wdThis.wdFirePlugToConfirmation();
  //@@end
}
```
Listing 3.13 Modified onActionRejectClicked() Method

3. The confirmation screen displays a summary of the absence notification once again and asks if the user is sure about the decision just made. The question is constructed in the Component Controller method createConfirmQuestion(), which you should create and implement as shown in Listing 3.14.

```
public void createConfirmQuestion( )
{
  //@@begin createConfirmQuestion()
  String approvalState;

  if (APPROVED.equals(wdContext
            .currentContextElement()
            .getApprove_reject_flag()))
    approvalState = "approval";
```

```
    else
        approvalState = "rejection";

    String confirmQuestion = "Please confirm
        your "+approvalState+" of this item:";

    wdContext.currentContextElement()
        .setConfirmQuestion(confirmQuestion);
    //@@end
}
```

Listing 3.14   createConfirmQuestion() Method of the Component Controller

4. Map the following context elements from the Component Controller to the `ConfirmApproval` view:
   ▶ `confirmQuestion`
   ▶ `detailOutput • Workitem_Detail • Wi_Text`
   ▶ `leave1`
   ▶ `leave1_visibility`
   ▶ `leave2`
   ▶ `leave2_visibility`
   ▶ `leave3`
   ▶ `leave3_visibility`
   ▶ `statusText`

5. Add elements to the `ConfirmApproval` view (see Table 3.9, Figure 3.17, and Figure 3.18).

View Element	Comments
RootUIElementContainer	Set the `layout` property to `GridLayout`.
ConfirmQuestionTextView	Set `text` property to the `confirmQuestion` element.
HeadingTextView	Bind the `text` property to the `Wi_Text` context element, and set the `design` property to `emphasized`.
Leave1TextView	Bind the `text` property to the `leave1` context element and the `visible` property to the `leave1_visibility` element.
Leave2TextView	Bind the `text` property to the `leave2` context element and the `visible` property to the `leave2_visibility` element.

Table 3.9   Elements of the ConfirmApproval View

View Element	Comments
Leave3TextView	Bind the `text` property to the `leave3` context element and the `visible` property to the `leave3_visibility` element.
ButtonContainer	This `TransparentContainer` element contains the `OKButton` and `CancelButton`.
OKButton	Set the `text` property to OK.
CancelButton	Set the `text` property to `Cancel`.
StatusTextView	Bind the `text` property to the `statusText` context element.

Table 3.9   Elements of the ConfirmApproval View (cont.)

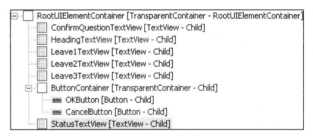

Figure 3.17   ConfirmApproval View Element Structure

Figure 3.18   ConfirmApproval in the View Designer

6. For the **OK** button's `onAction` property, create a new action `OKClicked`, which fires the `toResult` plug.

7. For the **Cancel** button's `onAction` property, create a new action `CancelClicked`, which fires the `toApproval` plug. This means that if the user clicks the **Cancel** button, no approval will take place, and the user will be taken back to the first screen.

Component Controller — Process Decision

With the first screens out of the way, the next part of the application deals with the user confirming the selection of the Approve or Reject options. These options are dealt with in the same way, the only difference being whether "A" or "R" is passed to SAP Business Workflow to approve or reject the item.

1. Create a method `processAbsence()` on the Component Controller.

2. Modify the `onActionOKClicked` method as shown in Listing 3.12. This method says that when a user clicks the **OK** button, the application processes the approval and then moves on to the result screen where the user will be informed of the completion of the decision.

3. Create the Component Controller method `process-Absence()`, and implement it as shown in Listing 3.16, along with the helper methods shown in Listing 3.17 (shown with comments only here; the full listing is shown in Appendix C).

```
public void onActionOKClicked(
    IWDCustomEvent wdEvent )
{
  //@@begin onActionApproveClicked(
      ServerEvent)
  wdThis.wdGetApproveAbsenceController()
      .processAbsence();
  wdThis.wdFirePlugToResult();
//@@end
}
```

Listing 3.15   Modified onActionApproveClicked() Method

```
public void processAbsence( )
{
  //@@begin processAbsence()
  logger.entering();
  StringBuffer bufStatus = new StringBuffer();

  // Get the necessary values from the Component Context
  String workitem_id = wdContext.currentContextElement().getWi_id();
  String approveRejectFlag = wdContext.currentContextElement().getApprove_reject_flag();
  String form_id = wdContext.currentContextElement().getForm_id();

  // Write the approval status to the form
  writeAbsForm(form_id, approveRejectFlag, getUserId(), new Date());

  // Write the approval status for the work item container
  HashMap elements = new HashMap();
  elements.put(_WI_RESULT, approveRejectFlag);
  elements.put(_RESULT, approveRejectFlag);

  // Complete the work item -> Committed, passing in the new container values
  completeWorkitem(workitem_id, elements);

  // Complete the work item -> Completed
  completeWorkitem(workitem_id, null);
```

Listing 3.16   processAbsence() Method of the Component Controller

54

```
// Create the status message for the final screen
String status = "The absence has been successfully ";
if (APPROVED.equals(approveRejectFlag))
    status += "approved.";
else
    status += "rejected.";
wdContext.currentContextElement().setStatusText(status);


logger.exiting();
//@@end
}
```

Listing 3.16 processAbsence() Method of the Component Controller (cont.)

```
private String getUserId()
{
  // Get the SAP user ID of the currently logged-in user
}


private void writeAbsForm(String form_id, String approveRejectFlag, String userId,
       Date approvalDate)
{
  // Call SWK_DEMO_FORMABS_PROC_WRITE with form_id, approval status, user ID,
  //   and date as inputs
}


private void completeWorkitem(String workitem_id, HashMap elements)
{
  // Call SAP_WAPI_WORKITEM_COMPLETE with workitem_id and container values as input
}
```

Listing 3.17 Helper Methods for processAbsence() (Comments Only)

Prepare Final View and Create Application
After the user makes the decision and submits it to SAP Business Workflow, the last part of building the application is to display the result of the decision on the final screen and then to construct a Web Dynpro application from the component you have been building.

1. Map the context element statusText from the Component Controller to the ShowResult view.

2. In the ShowResult view, set the defaultTextView's text property to the statusText context element.

3. Create an application AbsenceApproval in the Web Dynpro project, and check the box requiring **Authentication** (see Figure 3.19).

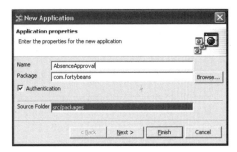

Figure 3.19 Creating the Web Dynpro Application Entry

Testing the Application from a Browser

Now that you've constructed the Web Dynpro Java project and application, you should build it and deploy it to a portal server and then set up the component's Web Dynpro Java Connector (JCo) destinations to point to the SAP Business Workflow system (**Content Administration • Web Dynpro • Maintain JCo Destinations**). To test the application, you'll need to generate an absence notification and find out the work item ID of the item in the approver's inbox. You can find this from UWL if you have support information turned on.

Tip: Enabling UWL Support Information

You can get a great deal of useful debugging information by setting the UWL iView property **Display UWL Support Information** (technical name `displaySupport`) to **Yes**. The **Current Item Information** section includes the work item ID for the item currently selected in the UWL (see Figure 3.20).

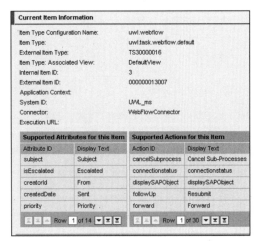

Figure 3.20 Work Item Support Information Showing the Item ID to be 13007

1. To get the URL of the application, navigate in the portal to **Content Administration • Web Dynpro**, and then drill down to find the application (see Figure 3.21). For our example project, the DC name is **local/AbsenceApproval**, and the application name is **AbsenceApproval**.

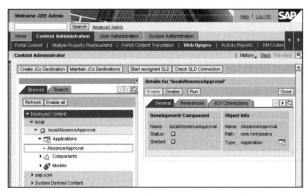

Figure 3.21 Locating a Web Dynpro Application

2. Click the **Run** button to launch the application in a new window. You should see a message saying there is no `wi_id` parameter.

3. You can fix this by adding "?wi_id=13007" to the URL (assuming the work item ID is 13007) and clicking the browser's **Go** button. You should then see the work item information displayed, as shown in Figure 3.22.

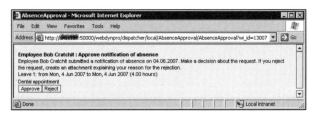

Figure 3.22 Running the Application in a Browser

Integrating the Application with UWL

Finally, to integrate this Web Dynpro application with UWL (as you saw in Chapter 2), proceed with the following steps:

1. In the SAP Business Workflow system, run transaction SWFVISU and create a Web Dynpro Java entry for task type `TS30000016` (see Figure 3.23).

2. Create visualization parameters for this entry:

   ▶ `APPLICATION` should be the application name (`AbsenceApproval`).

   ▶ `PACKAGE` should be the DC name (`local/AbsenceApproval`).

▶ SYSTEM_ALIAS should be SAP_LocalSystem (reflecting the fact that the application runs on the portal server).

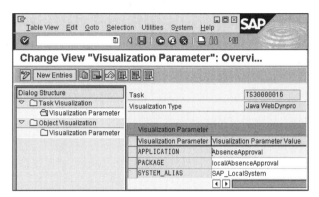

Figure 3.23   SWFVISU Settings for the Web Dynpro Application

3. Re-register the system by navigating in the portal to **System Administration • System Configuration • Universal Worklist & Workflow • Universal Worklist –**

Administration and clicking the **Re-Register** button for the SAP Business Workflow system entry.

4. Create a notification of absence, and then log in to the portal as the approver. Click on the corresponding work item, and the Web Dynpro application should be launched, as shown in Figure 3.24.

Workshop 2: Java iView Application Item Handler

You don't have to use Web Dynpro to process work items; the older Java iView technology, using HTML Business (HTMLB), can also be used. In some situations, this can be a more flexible technology because it allows you to mix HTMLB elements with native HTML. This means that a designer can create the look and feel using standard web design tools, and this can then be integrated by a developer to display the information in the correct places.

In this workshop, you will see how to create the HTMLB/JSPDynPage version of the Web Dynpro application shown previously.

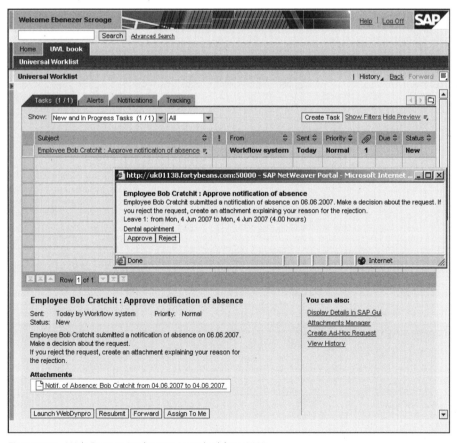

Figure 3.24   Web Dynpro Application Launched from UWL

Creating the Project in the NWDS
Before you start writing code, you must first create and configure a suitable project from the Enterprise Portal perspective.

1. Navigate to **Window • Open Perspective • Other...**, and then select **Enterprise Portal**.
2. Navigate to **File • New Project...**, select a **Development Component Project,** and click **Next**.
3. Select the Software Component **Local Development • My Components,** and click **Next**.
4. Enter a name for the project (in this example, "absncapp"), select the component type **Portal Application Module,** and click **Next** (see Figure 3.25). Portal application components are used for developing Java iViews.

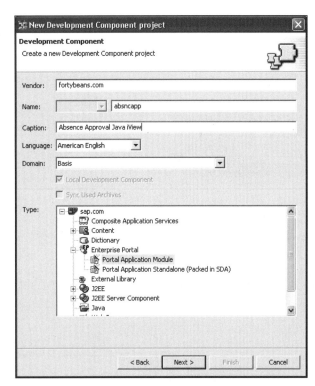

Figure 3.25 Creating a DC Project for the iView

5. Accept the default option to create an empty project with the archive name `absncapp.par`, and click **Finish**.
6. With the "absncapp" project selected, navigate to **File • New • Other • Portal Application**, select **Create a new Portal Application Project,** and then click **Next**.
7. Select the `absncapp` project, and click **Next**.
8. Choose the template **Portal Component • JSPDynPage,** and click **Next**.

9. Fill in the component name, (automatically copied to the **JSPDynPage class name**), package name, and JSP file name (see Figure 3.26), and then click **Next**.

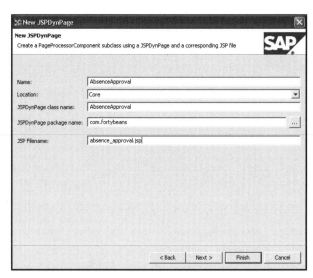

Figure 3.26 Specifying the Generated JSPDynPage Template

10. Select the option to **Generate bean statements**, fill in the bean and class names (see Figure 3.27) making sure you set the bean scope to **session**, and then click **Finish**.

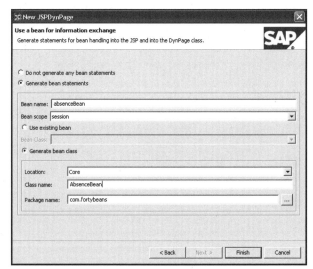

Figure 3.27 Specifying the Bean Properties

Create a Development Component for Portal Services
Now that you've created the basic portal component project, you also need to create a development compo-

nent for calling RFCs using the JCA (Java Connector Architecture) service, as follows:

1. Create another DC using the preceding steps 1 to 3, but this time, select an **External Library** component type named **prtlsvcs** (see Figure 3.28).

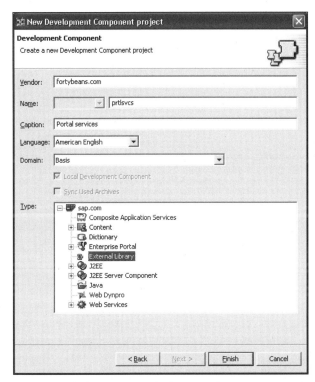

Figure 3.28 Creating an External Library Development Component

2. Copy the following files to the `libraries` folder of the `prtlsvcs` DC (from your SAP NetWeaver AS Java installation):

   ▶ `j2ee\cluster\server0\apps\sap.com\irj\ servlet_jsp\irj\root\WEB-INF\portal\porta- lapps\com.sap.portal.ivs.connectorservice\ lib\com.sap.portal.ivs.connectorservice_ api.jar`

   ▶ `j2ee\cluster\server0\bin\ext\com.sap.por- tal.services.api\portal_services_api_ lib.jar`

3. Navigate to **Window • Open Perspective • Other...**, and then select **Development Configurations**.

4. In the **Local DCs** pane, drill down to **Local Development • MyComponents • services • DC MetaData • Public Parts**, then right-click, and select **New Public Part...** (see Figure 3.29).

5. Create a public part named **PortalServices** of type compilation (see Figure 3.30) and then click **Finish**, but do *not* add the JAR files from this dialog box.

Figure 3.29 Create a New Public Part for a DC

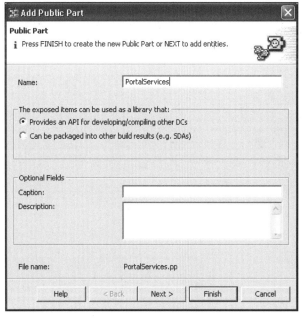

Figure 3.30 Specifying the Public Part for the DC

6. Go to the portal perspective. In the Navigator view (a tab at the bottom of the screen), select each JAR file. Open the context menu, and choose **Development Component • Add to Public Part** (see Figure 3.31). Choose the `PortalServices` part just created, and then click **Finish**.

7. Finally, build this DC by right-clicking on it and selecting **Development Component • Build**.

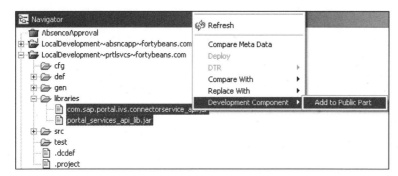

Figure 3.31 Adding the Library as a Public Part

Add Used DCs to the Portal Component

The last part of setting up the portal component project is to tell it which other components, libraries, and services will be used.

1. Switch to the Development Configurations Perspective (click the 🌀 icon), drill down to **Local Development • MyComponents • absncapp • DC MetaData • DC Definition • Used DCs**, right-click, and select **Add Used DC** (see Figure 3.32).

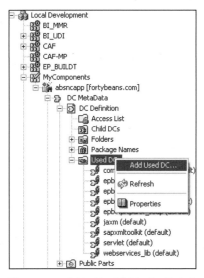

Figure 3.32 Add a Used DC to the Project

2. Add the following DCs:
   ▶ **Local Development • SAP-JEE •** tc/logging [sap.com]
   ▶ **Local Development • SAP-JEE •** j2eeca [sap.com]
   ▶ **Local Development • SAP_JTECHS •** tc/conn/connectorframework [sap.com]
   ▶ **Local Development • MyComponents •** prtlsvcs [fortybeans.com]

3. Go to the Enterprise Portal perspective, open the file dist/PORTAL-INF/portalapp.xml, and add the following line after the reference to com.sap.portal.htmlb:

```
<property name="PrivateSharingReference"
  value="com.sap.portal.ivs.connectorservice"
/>
```

Implementing the Component Code

Now that the project is set up, it's time to start writing the code to handle the work item. The best way to do this is to get the project from the SAP PRESS website for this book. For now, we'll just look at how things work rather than listing every single method.

Each of the following steps takes you through the flow of execution, from initial display of the work item details, to processing the user's input, to sending the decision to the SAP Business Workflow system and finally reporting the result of the decision.

1. The doInitialization() method shown in Listing 3.18 is called when the iView is launched from UWL.

```
public void doInitialization() {
  IPortalComponentSession componentSession =
    ((IPortalComponentRequest) getRequest())
        .getComponentSession();
  absenceBean = new AbsenceBean();
  componentSession.putValue(
        "absenceBean", absenceBean);
  // Populate the bean
  getItemDetails();
}
```

Listing 3.18 doInitialization() Method for JSPDynPage

The doInitialization() method calls getItem-Details() (see Listing 3.19), which populates the properties of absenceBean via the RFC-calling methods getWorkitemDetail(), getWorkitemDescription(), and getFormDetails(). These methods do the same job as their namesakes in the Web Dynpro workshop in the previous section. Listing 3.20 shows the comments for the methods to remind you what they do.

```
void getItemDetails() {
    String status = new String();
    String workitem_id =
        ((IPortalComponentRequest) getRequest()).getParameter("wi_id");
    absenceBean.setWi_id(workitem_id);

    if (workitem_id == null) {
        absenceBean.setStatusText("Error: no wi_id parameter.");
        absenceBean.setButtonVisible(false);
        return;
    }

    // Get the workitem detail & description from SAP Business Workflow
    //  using SAP_WAPI_GET_WORKITEM_DETAIL and SAP_WAPI_WORKITEM_DESCRIPTION
    getWorkitemDetail(workitem_id);
    String description = getWorkitemDescription(workitem_id);
    absenceBean.setDescription(description);

    // Get the form ID using SAP_WAPI_GET_OBJECTS
    String formId = getFormId(workitem_id);
    absenceBean.setForm_id(formId);

    // Get the form details and set the context values for leave[1-3] and reason
    //  using SWK_DEMO_FORMABS_READ
    getFormDetails(formId);

    // If the work item is already completed, don't show the approve/reject buttons
    if (STATUS_COMPLETED.equals(absenceBean.getWi_stat())) {
        status += "This item has already been processed.\n";
        absenceBean.setButtonVisible(false);
    } else {
        absenceBean.setButtonVisible(true);
    }
```

Listing 3.19   getItemDetails() Method for JSPDynPage

```
        // Add a warning if there are any attachments to the work item
        if (absenceBean.getNumAttachments() > 0) {
            status += "This item has attachments - these cannot be viewed here.\n";
        }


        absenceBean.setStatusText(status);
}
```

Listing 3.19   getItemDetails() Method for JSPDynPage (cont.)

```
private void getWorkitemDetail(String workitem_id)
{
        // Call SAP_WAPI_GET_WORKITEM_DETAIL with workitem_id as input
        // Retrieve note_count, wi_stat, and wi_text from the RFC call output
}


private String getFormId(String workitem_id)
{
        // Call SAP_WAPI_GET_OBJECTS with workitem_id as input

        // Retrieve Typeid and Instid from the RFC output, as formType and formNumber

        // If the form type is an absence form, return the form number.
        // Otherwise, report an error.
}


private String getWorkitemDescription(String workitem_id)
{
        // Call SAP_WAPI_WORKITEM_DESCRIPTION with workitem_id as input
        // Build up a description line by line from the RFC Text_Lines table
        // Return the description as a string
}


private void getFormDetails(String form_id)
{
        // Call SWK_DEMO_FORMABS_READ with form_id as input

        // Build up description of the first leave entry from RFC output values
        // Firstday1, Lastday1, and Abshours1

        // Build up description of the second leave entry from RFC output values
```

Listing 3.20   Helper Methods for getItemDetails() (Comments Only)

```
    // Firstday2, Lastday2, and Abshours2

    // Build up description of the third leave entry from RFC output values
    // Firstday3, Lastday3, and Abshours3

    // Get the reason for absence from the RFC output
}
```

Listing 3.20 Helper Methods for getItemDetails() (Comments Only) (cont.)

2. The bean class `AbsenceBean` shown in Listing 3.21 is used to store information about the absence and the decision in between calls to the application. For brevity, only the member variables are shown in the listing; in actual fact, there is a `get()` and `set()` method for each variable.

```
public class AbsenceBean
  implements Serializable {
    private String wi_id;
    private String user_id;
    private String form_id;
    private String approveRejectFlag;
    private String description;
    private String statusText;
    private String leave1;
    private String leave2;
    private String leave3;
    private String reason;
    private boolean buttonVisible;
    private String wi_text;
    private String wi_stat;
    private String confirmQuestion;
    private int numAttachments;
    private int page = APPROVAL_PAGE;

    public static final int APPROVAL_PAGE = 0;
    public static final int CONFIRM_PAGE = 1;
    public static final int RESULT_PAGE = 2;
}
```

Listing 3.21 AbsenceBean Properties

3. When initialization is done, `doProcessBeforeOutput()` is called (see Listing 3.22), which determines the JSP to show — by default, `approval.jsp` (see Listing 3.23).

```
public void doProcessBeforeOutput()
          throws PageException {
  switch (absenceBean.getPage()) {
    case AbsenceBean.APPROVAL_PAGE :
      this.setJspName("approval.jsp");
      break;
    case AbsenceBean.CONFIRM_PAGE :
      this.setJspName("confirmation.jsp");
      break;
    case AbsenceBean.RESULT_PAGE :
      this.setJspName("result.jsp");
      break;
  }
}
```

Listing 3.22 doProcessBeforeOutput() Method of JSPDynPage

4. The screen produced by `approval.jsp` is shown in Figure 3.33.

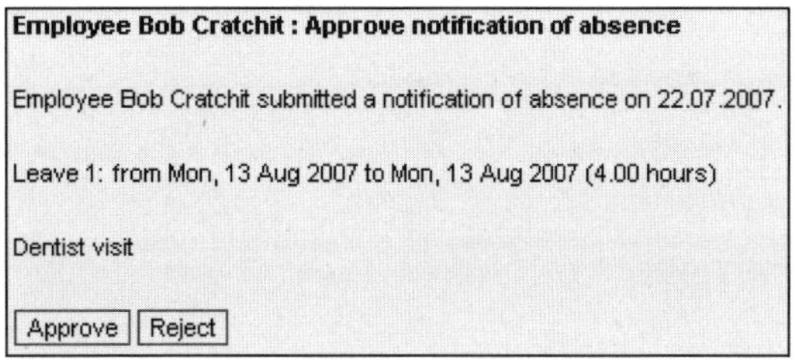

Figure 3.33 Sample Output from approve.jsp

```
<%@ taglib uri="tagLib" prefix="hbj" %>
<jsp:useBean id="absenceBean" scope="session" class="com.fortybeans.AbsenceBean" />
<hbj:content id="myContext" >
  <hbj:page title="PageTitle">
    <hbj:form id="myFormId" >
      <hbj:textView id="witext" design="EMPHASIZED"><%
             witext.setText(absenceBean.getWi_text());
      %></hbj:textView>
      <hbj:textView id="description" encode="false"><%
             description.setText(absenceBean.getDescription());
      %></hbj:textView>
      <p><hbj:textView id="leave1"><%
             leave1.setText(absenceBean.getLeave1());
      %></hbj:textView></p>
      <p><hbj:textView id="leave2"><%
             leave2.setText(absenceBean.getLeave2());
      %></hbj:textView></p>
      <p><hbj:textView id="leave3"><%
             leave3.setText(absenceBean.getLeave3());
      %></hbj:textView></p>
      <p><hbj:textView id="reason"><%
             reason.setText(absenceBean.getReason());
      %></hbj:textView></p>
      <% if (absenceBean.isButtonVisible()) {
      %><hbj:buttonRow>
             <hbj:button id="btnApprove" text="Approve" onClick="ClickApprove" />
             <hbj:button id="btnReject" text="Reject" onClick="ClickReject" />
         </hbj:buttonRow>
<%   } %>
      <p><hbj:textView id="statusText"><%
             statusText.setText(absenceBean.getStatusText());
      %></hbj:textView></p>
    </hbj:form>
  </hbj:page>
</hbj:content>
```

Listing 3.23   approval.jsp Displays Work Item Details

5. When a user clicks on the **Approve** or **Reject** buttons, the appropriate event handler method is run. onClickApprove() is shown in Listing 3.24. The onClickReject() method is identical, except that approveRejectFlag is set to REJECTED.

```
public void onClickApprove(Event event)
        throws PageException {
    absenceBean.setApproveRejectFlag(
        APPROVED);
    createConfirmQuestion();
```

```
absenceBean.setPage(
        AbsenceBean.CONFIRM_PAGE);
}
```

Listing 3.24 onClickApprove() Method for JSPDynPage

6. As with the Web Dynpro version of the application, no processing is done at this stage other than recording the user's decision and moving on to a screen asking the user to confirm the decision. The question asked is generated by the call to `createConfirmQuestion()`, shown in Listing 3.25.

```
void createConfirmQuestion() {
  String approvalState;

  if (APPROVED.equals(
        absenceBean.getApproveRejectFlag()))
    approvalState = "approval";
  else
    approvalState = "rejection";

  String confirmQuestion =
    "Please confirm your " + approvalState
      + " of this item:";

  absenceBean.setConfirmQuestion(
      confirmQuestion);
}
```

Listing 3.25 createConfirmQuestion() Helper Method

7. The confirmation screen `confirmation.jsp` is very similar to `approval.jsp` except that it contains **OK** and **Cancel** buttons in place of **Approve** and **Reject** buttons and also contains the approval question (see Figure 3.34).

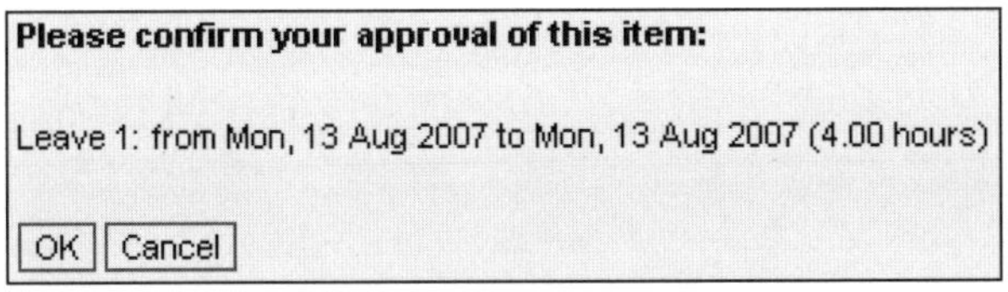

Please confirm your approval of this item:

Leave 1: from Mon, 13 Aug 2007 to Mon, 13 Aug 2007 (4.00 hours)

OK Cancel

Figure 3.34 Sample Output from confirmation.jsp

8. The **Cancel** button event handler sets the page back to `approval.jsp`; the **OK** button event handler

`onClickOK()` (see Listing 3.26) calls `processAbsence()` and sets the next page to be `result.jsp`.

```
public void onClickOK(Event event) throws
  PageException {

    processAbsence();
    absenceBean.setPage(AbsenceBean.RESULT_
PAGE);
}
```

Listing 3.26 onClickOK() Method of JSPDynPage

9. `processAbsence()` in turn calls SAP Business Workflow RFCs via the methods `writeAbsForm()` and `completeWorkItem()`, as shown in Listing 3.27.

```
void processAbsence() {
  StringBuffer bufStatus = new StringBuffer();

  // Get the necessary values from the bean
  String workitem_id = absenceBean.getWi_id();
  String approveRejectFlag =
        absenceBean.getApproveRejectFlag();
  String form_id = absenceBean.getForm_id();

  // Write the approval status to the form
  //  using SWK_DEMO_FORMABS_PROC_WRITE
  writeAbsForm(form_id, approveRejectFlag,
        getUserId(), new Date());

  // Complete the work item -> Committed,
  //  using SAP_WAPI_WORKITEM_COMPLETE
  //  with updated work item container elements
  HashMap elements = new HashMap();
  elements.put(_WI_RESULT, approveRejectFlag);
  elements.put(_RESULT, approveRejectFlag);
  completeWorkitem(workitem_id, elements);

  // Complete the work item -> Completed
  //  using SAP_WAPI_WORKITEM_COMPLETE
  completeWorkitem(workitem_id, null);

  // Create the status message
  String status =
        "The absence has been successfully ";
```

```
if (APPROVED.equals(approveRejectFlag))
  status += "approved.";
else
  status += "rejected.";

absenceBean.setStatusText(status);
}
```

Listing 3.27 processAbsence() Method Called from Event Handler

10. After `processAbsence()` has done its work, the user is taken to the final screen, `result.jsp` (see Listing 3.28), which informs the user of the success of the decision (see Figure 3.35).

```
<%@ taglib uri="tagLib" prefix="hbj" %>
<jsp:useBean id="absenceBean" scope="session"
      class="com.fortybeans.AbsenceBean" />
<hbj:content id="myContext" >
  <hbj:page title="PageTitle">
  <hbj:form id="myFormId" >
      <hbj:textView
          id="statusText"><%
          statusText.setText(
              absenceBean.getStatusText());
      %></hbj:textView>
  </hbj:form>
  </hbj:page>
</hbj:content>
```

Listing 3.28 result.jsp

The absence has been successfully approved.

Figure 3.35 Sample Output from result.jsp

Deploying the Application

After you've written (or copied) the code, you'll need to build the component and deploy it to the portal before you can try it out:

1. Right-click on the project, and select **Quick PAR Upload** as shown in Figure 3.36. This should bring up the **PAR Export** dialog box shown in Figure 3.37.

2. If you have not already done so, click the button **Configure servers settings...**, and enter the details of your portal server.

3. Make sure a password has been entered for the portal server, and then click the **Finish** button. This will build the component archive (if necessary) and deploy it to the portal.

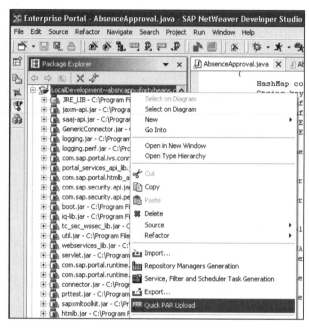

Figure 3.36 Menu for Deploying the PAR File

Figure 3.37 Dialog box for Deploying PAR File to Portal

4. Log in to the portal, and create a new iView, selecting the option to base the iView on a portal component (see Figure 3.38).

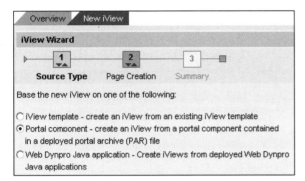

Figure 3.38 Create a New iView from a Portal Component

5. Choose the recently deployed archive from the list of archives (absncapp in the example shown in Figure 3.39).

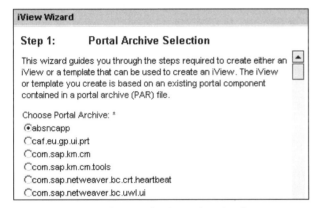

Figure 3.39 Choose the Entry for the Deployed Archive

6. Choose the relevant (usually the only) component from the archive (see Figure 3.40).

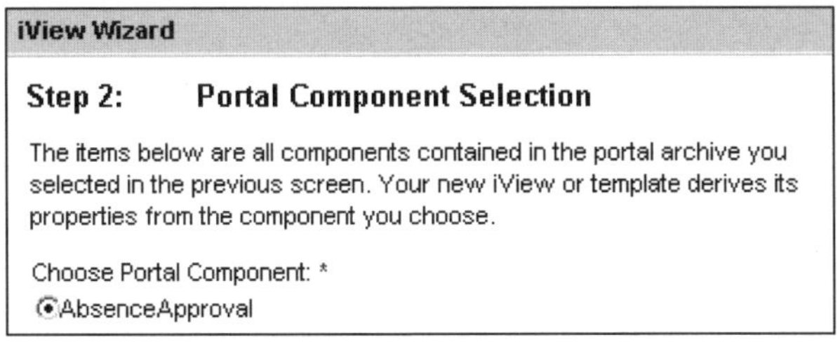

iView Wizard

Step 2:   Portal Component Selection

The items below are all components contained in the portal archive you selected in the previous screen. Your new iView or template derives its properties from the component you choose.

Choose Portal Component: *
⊙AbsenceApproval

Figure 3.40 Choose the Component from the Archive

7. Fill in the name, ID, and description of the iView as usual (see Figure 3.41).

Figure 3.41 Fill in the iView Name, ID, and Description

Integrating the Application with UWL

Finally, integrate this iView with UWL (as described in more detail in Chapter 2):

1. In the SAP Business Workflow system, run transaction SWFVISU, and create an iView entry for task type TS30000016.

2. Create one visualization parameter for this entry (see Figure 3.42): ID should be the PCD URL (pcd:portal_content/UWL_Book/AbsenceApprovalPar).

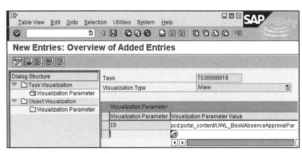

Figure 3.42 SWFVISU Settings for the iView

3. Re-register the system by navigating in the portal to **System Administration • System Configuration • Universal Worklist & Workflow • Universal Worklist – Administration** and clicking the **Re-Register** button for the SAP Business Workflow system entry.

4. Create a notification of absence (transaction SWXF), and then log in to the portal as the approver. Click on the corresponding work item, and the iView application should be launched, as shown in Figure 3.43.

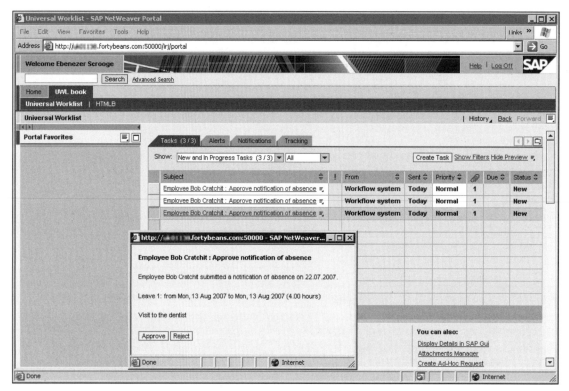

Figure 3.43   iView Launched from UWL

3.4   Summary

In this chapter, you've seen how to set up custom attributes in UWL and how to add them as columns to the worklist display. You've also learned how to customize work item behavior by enabling users to add memos and notes to items, adding decision buttons, and controlling which function modules get called in the SAP Business Workflow system using different action handlers. Finally, you saw how to write your own action handlers using Web Dynpro Java and Java iView technologies.

4 Other UWL Workflow Types

In Chapters 2 and 3, you saw how to work with SAP Business Workflow items in the portal using UWL. In this chapter you'll learn about the built-in features of UWL, such as the ad-hoc workflow (see Section 4.1) and the Knowledge Management (KM) publishing workflow (see Section 4.2), as well as how to extend the scope of UWL to model and execute new business processes directly in the SAP NetWeaver Portal (see Section 4.3) and how to work with tasks that do not necessarily come from a SAP Business Workflow back end (see Section 4.4).

4.1 Ad-hoc Workflow

Built into UWL is the ability for users to create their own informal workflows of one or more steps. These are not so much for standard, noncentralized processes (see Section 4.3), but they are for one-off instances of particular pieces of work to be done at the time. For example, a meeting might result in a number of actions, each of which could be created as an ad-hoc workflow task and assigned to one of the meeting's attendees.

Users create ad-hoc workflow tasks from the **Create Task** button in the **Tasks** tab of UWL (see Figure 4.1). Users can create ad-hoc tasks in five different ways, which we'll look at in detail next.

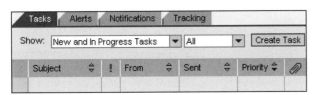

Figure 4.1 Button to Create an Ad-Hoc Workflow Task

Standalone Task

The Standalone task is the simplest task you can create. You enter a task description and assign the task to one or

more people (including roles and groups), with the option of having either a single task instance or one task instance per person. After an assignee marks the task as completed, it returns to the originator who can then approve or reject it.

As an example, let's say that Bob Cratchit and Ebenezer Scrooge both attended a meeting where they agreed that Bob would write up the minutes.

1. Ebenezer clicks the **Create Task** button in UWL and enters the details of the task, as shown in Figure 4.2.

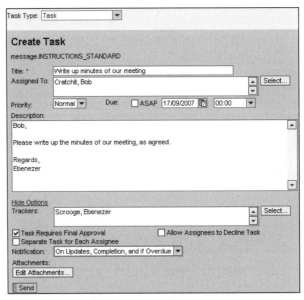

Figure 4.2 Creating a Simple Task

2. Clicking the **More Options** link shows the section in the lower third of the screen, and Ebenezer chooses to be notified of any changes to the task. The checkbox for **Task Requires Final Approval** enables Ebenezer to reject the minutes if he's not happy with them, meaning that Bob will have to do them again if they are not good enough.

3. After Ebenezer has created the task and clicked the **Send** button, the new task appears in Bob's UWL task list (see Figure 4.3).

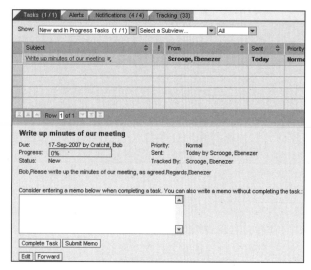

Figure 4.3 Task in Recipient's UWL

4. Bob writes up the minutes, as requested. If this were a simple offline task such as "Buy some coffee for the office kitchen," then Bob would just enter a comment and click the **Complete Task** button at this point. In our example though, Bob has been tasked with creating a document, so he clicks on the work item title instead to bring up the details page (see Figure 4.4).

5. Bob clicks the **Add Attachments...** button to upload his finished document and then clicks the **Complete Task** button.

Tip

To allow attachments on a task, you may need to configure portal security settings. Navigate to **System Administration • Permissions**, drill down to **Security Zones • sap.com • NetWeaver.KMC • low_safety**, and add a permission entry for the group **Everyone** to have **Read** permissions with the **End User** flag set.

6. After Bob has completed his task, it comes back to Ebenezer's UWL for approval, as shown in Figure 4.5.

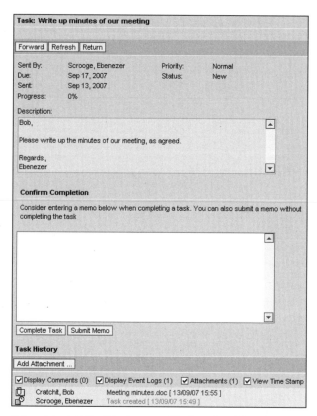

Figure 4.4 Add the Minutes as an Attachment and Complete the Task

7. Ebenezer can see the document by clicking on the link in the item preview and can then approve or reject it, with the option of entering a comment about the rejection.

8. On rejection, the item will go back to Bob (with progress reduced to 50 %), and Bob can look at the comment and have another go at the task.

9. When Ebenezer approves the task, it disappears from everyone's task list, although Ebenezer can review the item (in read-only mode) at any time via the UWL's Tracking tab.

Task List

Task List tasks, or multistep tasks, are simple business processes. As with the single Standalone task just described, any user can create a multi-step task, which can involve any other users. Unlike a single task, there are two types of steps in a multistep task, and the steps can be executed either one after the other (sequentially) or all at once (in parallel).

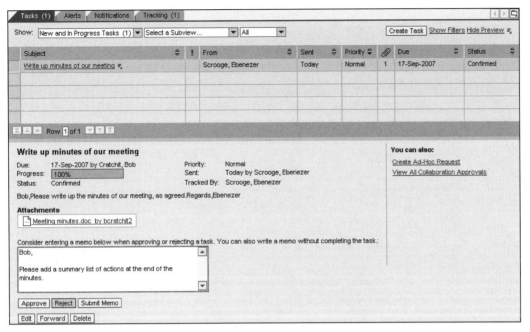

Figure 4.5   Task Comes Back to Originator for Approval

The step types are **Action Item** and **Approval**. An Action Item is just like a single task: A user does something and then confirms completion. An Approval task instead asks for an approve/reject decision from a user.

In Figure 4.6, you can see an example using both types of steps:

1. A project manager has asked a developer to create a change request for a new feature.
2. This change request needs to be approved by the project sponsor.
3. Once approved, the developer implements the change.

The individual steps in the task appear as items in each user's UWL as the sequence progresses. In Figure 4.7, you can see the details of the task in the developer's worklist after the first two steps have been carried out. At the top-right of the image, you can see the process summary showing the first two steps being successful, and at the bottom of the image, you can see the detailed history of the task, showing the attached document and the feedback from the project sponsor.

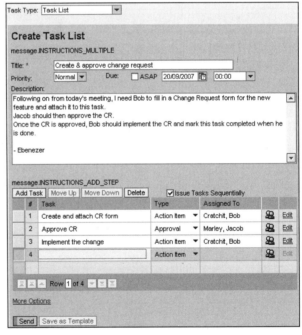

Figure 4.6   Create a Multistep Task

It's worth noticing that these users have just implemented and carried out a business process with nothing more than a few clicks. Merely by knowing how to create multistep tasks in UWL, end users can implement a lot of processes that might previously have required the expense of a SAP Business Workflow developer or the inefficiency of an email-based solution. In Section 4.3,

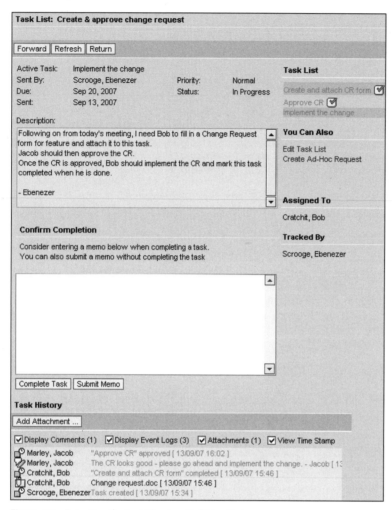

Figure 4.7   Executing the Last Step in a Multistep Task

you will see that with a little more training, a business process expert (BPX) can use Guided Procedures to do even more.

Workflow-Related Task (Subprocess)

Portal-based Task List tasks such as those you just learned about can be attached to existing work items from the SAP Business Workflow. Let's take the absence approval scenario from Chapter 3 as an example.

1. The workflow task will arrive in Ebenezer Scrooge's task list for a decision, but suppose that Bob Cratchit is also working on a project for another manager, Jacob Marley. Scrooge will want to make sure that Marley is also okay with the leave request.

2. All Scrooge has to do is click on the link **Create Ad-Hoc Request** from the task overview, and he can then delegate approval to Marley, as shown in Figure 4.8.

Tip: Display Link to Business Object

When the **Display Link To Business Object** checkbox is checked, the users in the subprocess can access the original absence notification form in the SAP Business Workflow back end system. However, this checkbox only appears if you configure the portal workflow engine to show it. The configuration is at **System Administration • System Configuration • Universal Worklist & Workflow • Workflow • Engine • Engine**. Set the property **Enable Link To Business Object** to **True**.

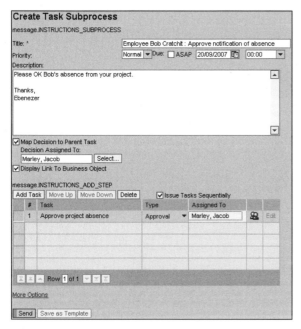

Figure 4.8 Creating a Subprocess

3. When Marley gives his approval for Bob's absence, the setting **Map Decision to Parent Task** means that his decision will be applied to the original workflow task in the SAP Business Workflow back end.

Request for Feedback

A Request for Feedback task does pretty much what it says: The initiator can ask a group of people for feedback on an issue. In the example shown in Figure 4.9, this means asking a team whether they think a Wiki would be a good idea. There are a couple of useful options:

▶ **Anonymous Responses**

The initiator can receive feedback without knowing who sent it.

▶ **Include Quick Response Option**

Adds a dropdown field for responders to quickly indicate their level of agreement on a scale from **Strongly Disagree** to **Strongly Agree**.

The task is complete when all the recipients have replied, though there is an option to make the task complete when only a certain number of people have replied. You can see the available options in Figure 4.9.

The recipient's view of the task is shown in Figure 4.10. As with other ad-hoc tasks, the recipient sees this view by clicking on the title of the work item from UWL.

You can see the recipient choosing from one of the **Quick Response** options, and you can see from the **Task History** at the bottom of the screen that one of the recipients has already replied.

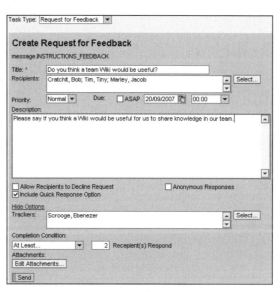

Figure 4.9 Creating a Request for Feedback

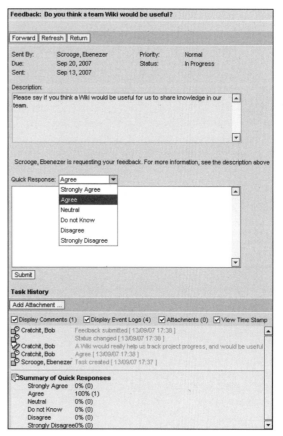

Figure 4.10 Recipient's View of a Request for Feedback

Request for Nomination

The final kind of ad-hoc task, the Request for Nomination, allows a user to request that a group of users (nominators) put forward the names of another group of users (nominees). For example, a department head might ask their managers for a list of conference attendees; Jacob Marley is asking Ebenezer Scrooge to do just this in Figure 4.11.

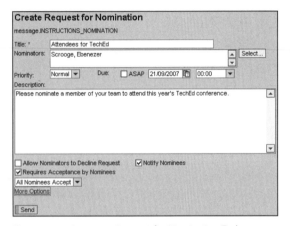

Figure 4.11   Creating a Request for Nomination Task

The checkboxes to notify nominees and require their acceptance mean that when Ebenezer nominates someone to go to the conference, they get a task like the one in Figure 4.12 requesting approval of their nomination.

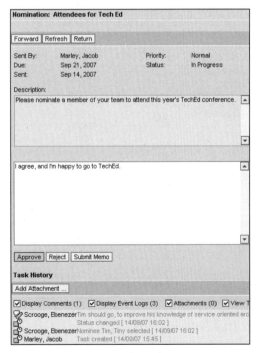

Figure 4.12   Nominee Accepting the Nomination

In newer releases of the SAP NetWeaver Portal, there is also the option to create a user group from the successful nominees, which can form the basis of ongoing collaboration. Perhaps the nominees get back from the conference and work together on a report of their experiences. They may want to publish this report for everyone in their organization to see, and for that they will need to use a publishing workflow, which is the subject of the next section.

4.2   Publishing Workflow

The portal's Knowledge Management (KM) system has a built-in publishing workflow that allows document authors to submit files for approval by one or more editors before they are visible to end users. Once published, documents can eventually be archived off so that users can no longer see them, but they are still accessible to authors and approvers. A summary of this process is shown in Figure 4.13.

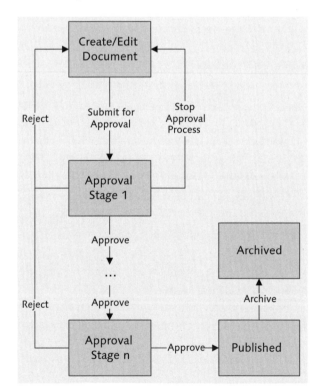

Figure 4.13   Portal KM Publishing Workflow

UWL is automatically integrated (i.e., no configuration necessary on your part) with this process in several ways:

▶ When a document reaches a given approval stage, an item is placed in the UWL Tasks list of each possible approver for that stage; as soon as one approver makes a decision, the task is removed from the worklists of all the others.

▶ When a document is either rejected or published, a notification is sent to the author's UWL Notifications list.

▶ Whenever a user sends Feedback on a document, a notification about the feedback is created in the author's UWL.

Configuring an Approval Workflow

To set up an approval workflow, you need to turn on Approvals for a given folder. All documents created in that folder, or any subfolders, must then be submitted and approved before they are visible to end users.

As an example, let's set up a two-stage process with a first stage of "Initial Review" and a second stage of "Final Publication." In this example, Bob Cratchit will create a document that anyone with the role "Initial Reviewer" will review and approve; Ebenezer Scrooge will then do a final check before the document gets published to end users, represented in this case by Tiny Tim. This process is shown graphically in Figure 4.14.

1. Make sure the portal roles **Author**, **Editor**, and **Initial Reviewer** exist by navigating to **Content Administration • Portal Content** and creating them in the PCD. Go to **User Administration • Identity Management**, and assign the **Author** role to Bob Cratchit, the **Initial Reviewer** role to Jacob Marley, and the **Editor** role to both Ebenezer Scrooge and Jacob Marley.

2. Create a folder called **Company News** in the **KM Public Documents** folder.

3. To activate approvals on this folder, bring up the **Details** screen from the folder's context menu (see Figure 4.15), go to **Settings • Approval** on the **Details** screen (see Figure 4.16), and click the button **Enable Approval Process** (see Figure 4.17). You will see a warning message about permissions, but don't worry about that right now because you'll fix the permissions in a few steps time, after defining the workflow.

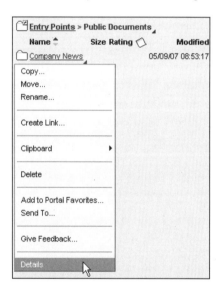

Figure 4.15   Accessing the Details Menu of a Folder

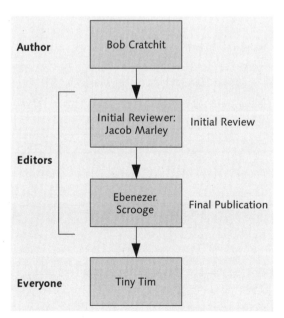

Figure 4.14   Example Publishing Approval Process

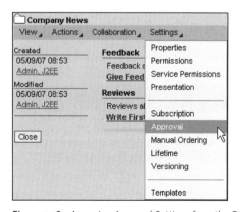

Figure 4.16   Accessing Approval Settings from the Detail Screen

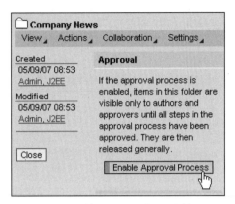

Figure 4.17   Enabling Approval on a Folder

4. Enter a name for the single step being shown — call it "Initial Review."

5. In the User Selection section of the screen, enter the name of the role, **Initial Reviewer**, and click the button **Add Approver to Step**. You will see the role icon and role name appearing next to the step.

6. Click the **Add Step** button and give the new step the name "Final Publication."

7. Enter "Scrooge" into the **User Selection** section of the screen and click **Add Approver to Step**. You will see the user icon and the name Ebenezer Scrooge appearing next to the step. The **Approval Process** screen should now look like Figure 4.18.

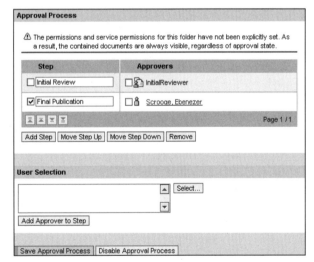

Figure 4.18   Approval Process Definition

8. Click the button **Save Approval Process.**

9. Set the folder permissions **Settings • Permissions** from the **Details** screen. Set the group **Everyone** to have **Read** permissions (i.e., *not* the default of **Full Control**).

Set the **Author** role to have **Full Control**, and the **Editor** role to have **Read/Write**, as shown in Figure 4.19.

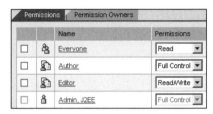

Figure 4.19   Folder Permissions for Approval Workflow

10. Similarly, ensure that the folder's service permissions (**Settings • Service Permissions**) are *not* set to give **Full Control** to **Everyone**. A safe default is for **Everyone** to have **Subscribe (Myself Only)**.

Tip

When setting the permissions, make sure you click the **Save Permissions** button before moving to another screen or section, or you will lose your changes with no warning.

Also, remember that the user who sets the permissions will automatically get **Full Control**, so make sure that the user doing the configuration is not one of the users who will be involved in the publishing process.

Running Through the Publishing Process

Now that you've configured this simple publishing workflow, it's time to create, publish, and get feedback on a document to see how the process works and how it interacts with UWL. All of the users involved with this process have the **Control Center User** portal role, which gives access to the **Public Documents** folder via **Home • Overview • Documents**, but any role that gives access to the relevant **KM** folder will do the job.

Create Document and Submit for Approval

In the following steps, Bob Cratchit will create a new document and submit it for approval.

1. Log in to the portal as Bob Cratchit, and create a new HTML file, as shown in Figure 4.20.

2. Give the file a name, and enter some content (see Figure 4.21). Note the spelling error ("bookeeping" should be "bookkeeping"), which should be picked up by an editor during approval.

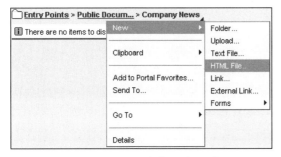

Figure 4.20 Creating a New File for Online Editing

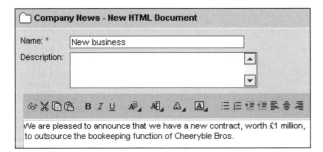

Figure 4.21 Name and Content for New File

3. **Save** the document.

4. Bring up the **Details** screen for the newly created document, and select the link **Submit for Approval**. You will see a confirmation message, and the link will change to **Stop Approval Process** (see Figure 4.22).

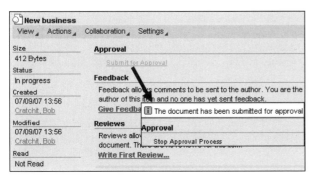

Figure 4.22 Submitting the Document for Approval

Rejection, Notification, and Resubmission

Now the document is in the approval process, so it's time for the editors to get involved.

1. Log in as Jacob Marley (who is an **Initial Reviewer**).

2. Jacob's UWL has a new task from Bob Cratchit, asking him to review the new document.

3. Click the **Display Item** button to launch the document in a new window so that you can review it.

4. Back in UWL, enter some feedback about the need to correct the spelling mistake, and click the **Reject** button (see Figure 4.23).

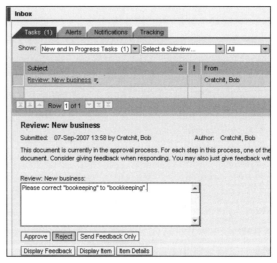

Figure 4.23 Item in Initial Reviewer's Inbox

5. Now that the document has been rejected, you need to go back to Bob Cratchit's portal to see the effect of the rejection.

6. Select the **Notification** tab of Bob Cratchit's UWL.

7. You should see two new items. One of these is the notification of rejection, mentioning the reviewer's feedback (see Figure 4.24); the other is the (slightly redundant) feedback item itself. The KM approval process treats the rejection and the feedback as two distinct actions.

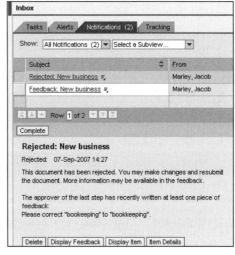

Figure 4.24 Notification of Feedback and Rejection in Author's UWL

8. As Bob Cratchit, go back and edit the document (**Edit Online** from the document's context menu) to correct the spelling mistake.

9. Bring up the **Details** screen for the document. Click on the **Feedback** link to bring up the list of feedback for the document, from which you can now delete the item about the spelling mistake.

10. You can now submit the document for approval once again. This time, try doing it from the **Actions** menu of the details screen by selecting **Actions • Approval • Submit for Approval**, as shown in Figure 4.25.

Figure 4.25   Resubmit from the Actions Menu

End-User Subscription

Before going on to approve the changed document, let's take a small diversion to log in as the end user, Tiny Tim. In this diversion, you'll verify that Tim cannot yet see the document being approved, and you'll set up a subscription to the folder so that Tim is notified when any new documents appear.

1. Logged in as Tiny Tim, navigate to **Home • Overview • Documents • Entry Points • Public Documents • Company News**. You will see, as in Figure 4.26, that there are no documents visible; the document in the approval process cannot yet be seen.

2. Bring up the **Details** page for the **Company News** folder, and select **Settings • Subscription** (see Figure 4.27).

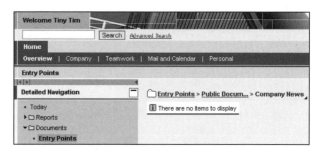

Figure 4.26   Document in Approval Is Not Yet Visible to Users

Figure 4.27   Accessing the Subscription Page

3. Configure the subscription to notify **Any Change** and to send notifications **On Every Event** (see Figure 4.28).

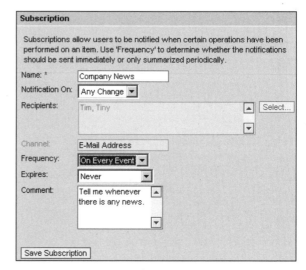

Figure 4.28   Setting Up a Subscription

Approval for Publication

Now that you've verified for Tiny Tim that unpublished documents can't be seen and asked to be notified of any changes to the folder, it's time to go back to the approval process.

1. Go to Jacob Marley's portal. You will see a UWL inbox item for the resubmitted document. This time, click the **Approve** button.

2. Log in to the portal as Ebenezer Scrooge, the final approver. You will see a UWL task from Jacob Marley (the previous approver) requesting a review of the document (see Figure 4.29). After reviewing the document, click the **Approve** button.

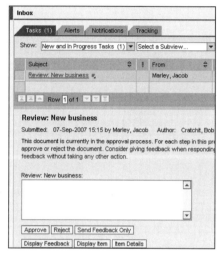

Figure 4.29   Item in Final Approver's UWL

3. Because this is the final step in the approval chain, the document will now be published for all users to see.

4. Go to Tiny Tim's portal. You will now see in Tiny Tim's UWL, a task highlighting that a new document has been published (see Figure 4.30). The item is listed as "From" Tiny Tim because it was Tim who set up the subscription.

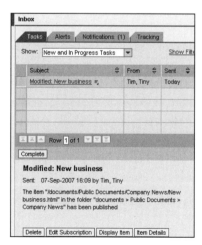

Figure 4.30   End User Gets Subscription Notification

5. Navigate to **Home • Overview • Documents • Entry Points • Public Documents • Company News** as Tiny Tim. You can see that the newly published document is visible (see Figure 4.31).

Figure 4.31   End User Can Now See the Document

6. Tiny Tim can even see how the document went through the approval process by bringing up the details screen for the document and selecting **Settings • Approval** (see Figure 4.32).

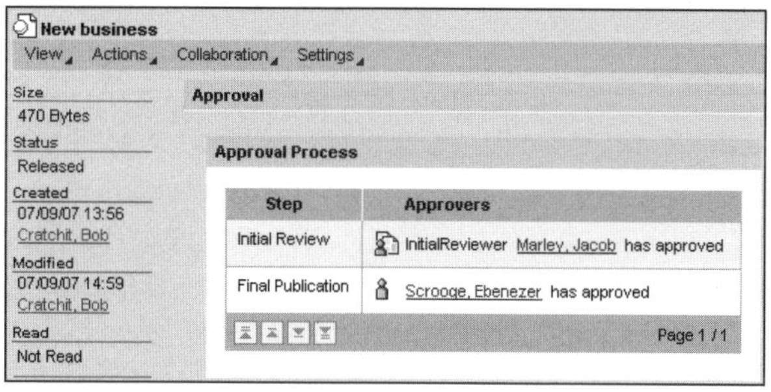

Figure 4.32   Settings • Approval Shows Approval History

4.3   Guided Procedures

Guided Procedures (GPs) are used to decentralize business processes by allowing business users to define and deploy processes on their own. GPs are intended to be repeatable processes, running across multiple back end systems or no back end system. They are intended for simple processes that do not require dedicated technical workflow expertise to set up and monitor.

In terms of complexity, GPs sit somewhere between collaboration tasks (ad-hoc workflow) in the portal and the SAP Business Workflow engine in ABAP-based systems. The advantage that GPs have over both is the ease with which they can interoperate with other systems in the landscape; this is one of the key benefits of a service-oriented architecture.

One of the downsides of GPs (for now, at least) is that it's harder to work with an organizational structure. SAP Business Workflow makes it easy to say "escalate this item to a person's manager for a decision"; GPs, like ad-hoc workflow, uses UME instead. This means you can easily set up processes that work with known individuals or portal roles/groups, but it's a bit more challenging to work with an organizational structure (you need either SAP ERP HCM or a call to a specific function module to find out someone's manager in GPs, whereas SAP Business Workflow can use an organization structure without requiring SAP ERP HCM).

Therefore, unless you're careful, if a manager of a department leaves the company, any GP (and ad-hoc) processes with which that manager was involved need to be reconfigured to work with someone else instead. For all that, GPs are still flexible tools for quickly putting together local, informal business processes.

Following is a simple example of creating a process in GPs, but we're only going to scratch the surface of what's really possible with this technology because it would require a book in itself to treat the subject properly.[1] However, there is a very good guide on the SAP Community Network, "Usage Guide for Guided Procedures on SAP NetWeaver 7.0" (for the link, see Table B.3 in Appendix B).

Process Overview

In this workshop, we return to the absence approval scenario, but this time with a twist. Instead of using SAP Business Workflow, we will use a GP to model a simplified version of the same process. The end result will be similar — a populated FORMABSENC business object will appear in the SAP Business Workflow system when the absence is approved — but the process itself will be carried out in GPs in the portal, with the last step being to create the FORMABSENC object. Figure 4.33 shows the process flow.

A GP can be complex, being made up of a series of blocks (each being parallel or serial), with each block containing a number of actions, and each action referring to a callable object (CO), which actually carries out the pro-

cess step. For our example, we will use a single serial block for the process.

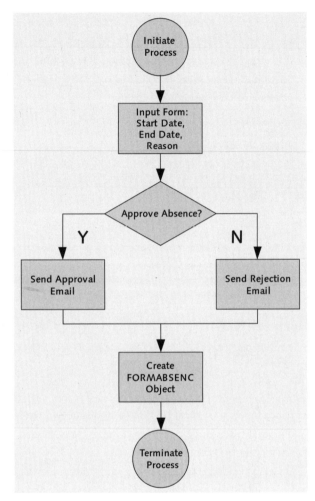

Figure 4.33 Absence Approval Process

SAP delivers a large variety of COs, and you can also write your own. COs are a bit like iViews in the portal in that you can have COs calling user interface elements such as SAP transactions, Web Dynpro applications, and so on. Unlike iViews, however, you can also have various "background processing" COs to help the process along; calling a RFC is an example of one such CO.

You can find a guide to using SAP-delivered COs at "Creating Callable Objects in the GP Design Time" in the SAP Help Portal (see Table B.3 in Appendix B for the link); for our simple process, we will be using just the objects listed in Table 4.1.

---

1 Such as *The Developer's Guide to the SAP NetWeaver Composition Environment* (SAP PRESS, 2008).

Type	Description
Simple Input Form	Provides an input form for arbitrary data based on the output parameter list.
Read User Information	Provides the capability to read user information based on the unique id, the logon id, or the current user.
Approval Callable Object	Approve or reject input data of the CO and send an email accordingly.
Business Logic	The business logic CO provides the ability to evaluate output parameters and result status using logical expressions based on its input parameters.
External Service (RFC Endpoint)	Calls a remote function module in a connected SAP system.

Table 4.1 Callable Object Types Used in Simple Process

Before you start, make sure that your user has the right portal roles; to design GPs, you will need the **GP Administrator**, **GP Business Expert,** and **GP Expert User** roles. To initiate or take part in a GP, you will also need the **GP**

User role. After you've got the right roles assigned, navigate to **Guided Procedures • Design Time** in the portal.

We'll kick off by creating the COs, then we'll create the actions from the COs, and finally we'll compose the actions into a block and create a process based on that block.

Create an Input Form Callable Object

So, COs first:

1. From the Design Time Gallery, select **Create Callable Object** (you might want to create a folder first, to put all bits and pieces for the process in).

2. Select the **Data Input Form** object type from the **Forms** section of the **Type** menu, enter a name and description for the CO (see Figure 4.34), and then click **Next**.

3. Insert context parameters for **Start Date**, **End Date,** and **Reason**, remembering that the **Start Date** and **End Date** parameters are of type Date. For the technical names of the parameters, just use the parameter name with any spaces removed, so "Start Date" becomes StartDate (see Figure 4.35).

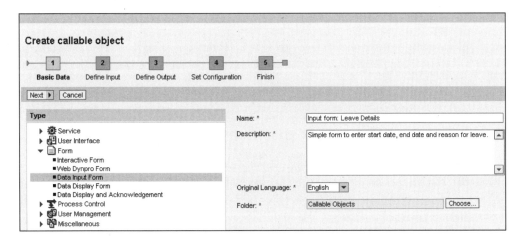

Figure 4.34 Start by Creating a Data Input Form CO

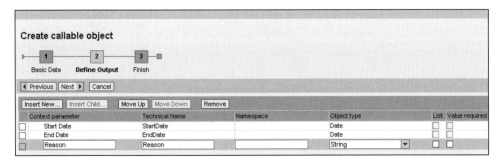

Figure 4.35 Set Up the Context Parameters for the Input Form

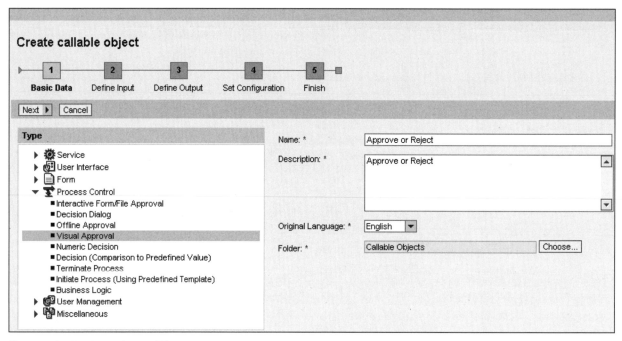

Figure 4.36 Creating an Approval Form

4. After you've set up the context parameters, click **Next**, then **Finish and Open**, and activate the object by clicking the ▯ icon (**Activate**).

Create an Approval Callable Object

Now you've done the input form, next up is the Approval CO:

1. Create another CO, this time of type **Visual Approval** from the **Process Control** section, and again give it a name and description before clicking **Next** (see Figure 4.36).

2. You want the approver to see the absence information, so add the context parameters for **Start Date**, **End Date,** and **Reason**. You also want to use the approver's name in an email sent by this step, so add context parameters for the approver's first and last names too. Later, you'll see how to populate these parameters and send the email, but for now, just make sure the parameters are there (see Figure 4.37), and then click **Next**.

3. In step 3 (**Define Output**), just accept the default output parameters, and click **Next**.

4. In step 4, leave the default email settings for now, click **Next**, and then click **Finish and Open**. Finally, click the **Activate** icon to activate the object.

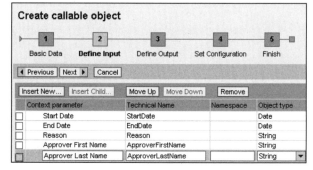

Figure 4.37 Context Parameters for Approval

Create Email Templates for Approval and Rejection

The next step is to define templates for the approval and rejection emails. After these are done, you can go back to the approval object and configure it to use these templates.

1. Navigate to **Guided Procedures • Administration** in the portal, and select **Maintain E-Mail Templates** from the **General** section (see Figure 4.38).

2. Click the link to create a new HTML template, and then enter a title and some text for this template. Do the approval template first (see Listing 4.1 and Figure 4.39).

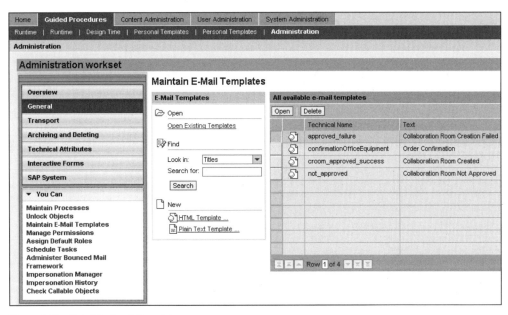

Figure 4.38 Maintain Email Templates

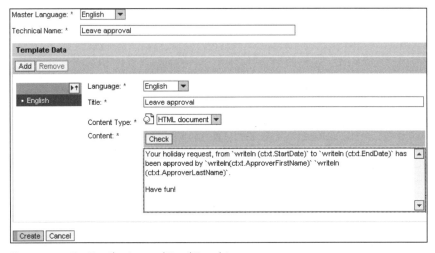

Figure 4.39 Creating the Approval Email Template

```
Your holiday request, from
`writeln (ctxt.StartDate)` to
`writeln (ctxt.EndDate)`
has been approved by
`writeln(ctxt.ApproverFirstName)`
`writeln(ctxt.ApproverLastName)`.

Have fun!
```

Listing 4.1 Email Template Text for Approval Email

The back-tick character (`) surrounds sections of script that allow you to write out the values of context parameters (those which are defined as inputs to the object referencing the template). The special name ctxt refers to the context, and you can also use sy and role to get access to system- and role-specific information, respectively. The SAP Help Portal section **Creating Composite Applications • Developing Composite Applications with CAF GP • Reference • Tutorials • Developing Your First Process • Setting Up Mail Templates • Replacements** gives more details on using these parameters.

3. Create a template for leave rejection in the same way but use different template text (see Listing 4.2).

```
Unfortunately, your holiday request, from
`writeln (ctxt.StartDate)` to
`writeln (ctxt.EndDate)` has been rejected by
`writeln(ctxt.ApproverFirstName)`
`writeln(ctxt.ApproverLastName)`.
```

Listing 4.2 Email Template Text for Rejection Email

4. Now that you've created the templates, it's time to go back to the approval CO to assign them. Go to **Guided Procedures • Design Time,** and navigate through the **Gallery** to find the approval CO you created in the previous section (see Figure 4.40).

Figure 4.40 Open the Approve or Reject Object Again

5. Click the icon (**Toggle Single Edit Mode**), and click **Yes** when asked "Do you want to update to inactive version?" Select the **Configuration** tab for the CO, select the appropriate templates, and set the recipient for both emails to be the **Initiator** (see Figure 4.41).

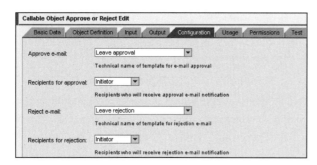

Figure 4.41 Fill in the Values for Email Templates and Recipients

This is because the person who requested the absence (the initiator of the process) needs to get the email informing the initiator of the decision.

6. At the top of the screen, click the ⬛ icon (**Activate**) to activate the object.

Create an RFC Callable Object

Now follow these steps to create the CO that will actually create the FORMABSENC object in the SAP Business Workflow system:

1. Before you create the CO itself, you need to go back to the **Guided Procedures • Administration** menu to configure the connection to the SAP Business Workflow system. Select **Configure End Points** from the **SAP System** menu (see Figure 4.42).

Figure 4.42 Location of the Configure End Points Menu

2. On the next screen, click the **Add...** button to go to a screen where you can define the properties of the SAP Business Workflow system, including the user name and password of a user with authorizations to call the RFC in question (see the following "Single Sign-On for Guided Procedure RFC Calls" box for an explanation).

Single Sign-On for GP RFCs

Note that you need to define the user name and password of a user in the SAP Business Workflow system. Single sign-on with logon tickets cannot work in a GP because the process step may be running in the background with no logged-in user, and logon tickets are only generated when a user logs in. The only ways to use single sign-on are the following:

▶ Specify an existing portal alias for a system configured for user mapping.

▶ Use X.509 client certificates for login.

In either of these cases, the GP can use the credentials of the user executing the process step even if the user is not actually logged in at the time the step is being executed.

In this case, we will set up the endpoint to always log in with a specified user instead of using user mapping because the RFC we will be calling allows us to specify the process user in its import parameters.

3. Enter the usual SAP system connection details (as in Chapter 2), click **Test** to make sure the connection is configured correctly, and then click **Save** (see Figure 4.43).

Add endpoint alias	
Endpoint Alias Name: *	SAP_Workflow
Endpoint Alias Type: *	Endpoint Alias for Remote Function Call (RFC)
Endpoint Alias Properties	
Connection Mode: *	Connection Defined by User
Client: *	100
User Name: *	j2ee_admin
Password: *	••••••••
Pool Size:	
Server Mode: *	Logon Group
SAP System Name: *	NSP
Message Server: *	workflow.fortybeans.com
Logon Group: *	PUBLIC
Security Network Communication (SNC): *	OFF
Portal Alias for SAP System:	GP_business_workflow

Test | Save | Cancel

Figure 4.43   Setting Up an SAP System as a GP Endpoint Alias

4. With the endpoint alias in place for connecting to the SAP Business Workflow system, now go back to **Guided Procedures • Design Time,** and create a CO of type **External Service** from the **Service** menu. Give the CO a name and description, and then click **Next** (see Figure 4.44).

5. From the **Logical Destination** dropdown, pick the endpoint alias you just created.

6. For the function name, enter "SWF_DEMO_FORMABS_CREATE" and for the function group, just enter a "*****" as a wildcard character (you may get an error message if you don't enter any data for **Function Group**). Click **Search** to bring back the matching RFC from the SAP Business Workflow system (see Figure 4.45).

7. Click the **Next** button until you get to the **Set Configuration** page (you can't change anything on the **Define Input** and **Define Output** pages), and change the error-handling mode to **No Error Handling** (see Figure 4.46) because the RFC being called does not support this feature.

8. Click **Next**, click **Finish and Open**, and then click (**Activate**) to activate.

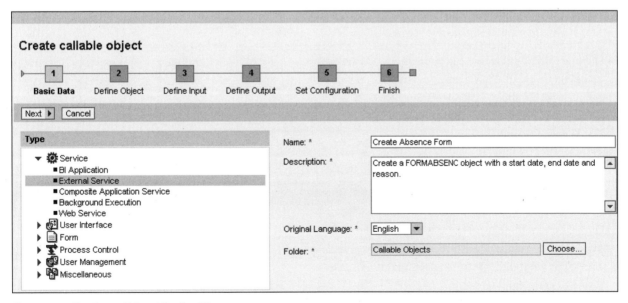

Figure 4.44   Creating an External Service CO

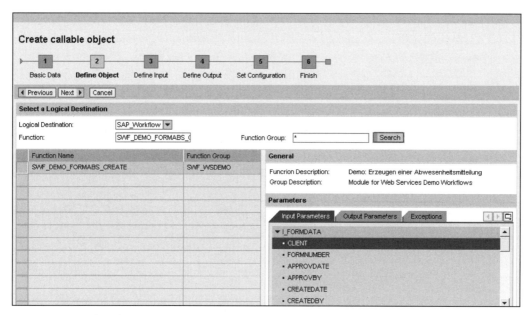

Figure 4.45   Searching for an SAP Remote-Enabled Function

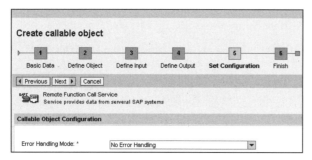

Figure 4.46   Turn Off Error Handling

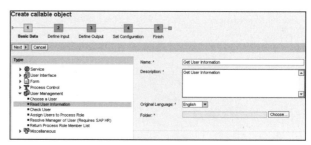

Figure 4.47   Creating a User Information CO

Callable Object to Get User Info

Now that you've created the main three COs for the process — an input form, an approval step, and an RFC call — there are a couple more COs you need to create to help glue things together. The first one is a CO you'll use to get information about a user, which will be used later to get information about the person filling in the form as well as the person approving it. This will be used in the email templates (where the approver's name is mentioned) and in the RFC call (the FORMABSENC object records the initiator and the approver of the request).

1. To create this CO, go to the Guided Procedures Design Time Gallery, and select **Read User Information** from the **User Management** section. Enter a name and description for the CO, and then click **Next** (see Figure 4.47).

2. Skip past the **Input** and **Output** pages (which can't be changed), and in the **Set Configuration** page, make sure the **Resolution Mode** is set to **Current User** (see Figure 4.48), which means that you will get the information about whichever user is executing the process step.

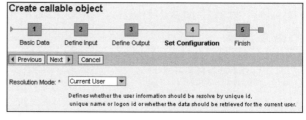

Figure 4.48   Set Resolution Mode to Current User

3. Click **Next**, **Finish and Open,** and then the ▯ icon (**Activate**) to activate the object.

Business Logic Objects

The next bit of glue is a pair of business logic COs. Business logic COs can evaluate input parameters and set output parameters according to logical expressions that you can define. We'll set up one of these to prepare FORMAB-SENC values following a rejection and another to prepare values following an approval.

1. To do the first of these, go to the Guided Procedures Design Time, and create a new CO of type **Business Logic** in the **Process Control** section (see Figure 4.49). Give the object a name and description, and then click **Next**.

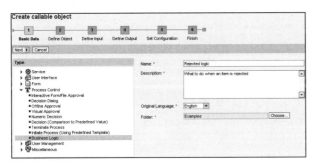

Figure 4.49 Creating a Business Logic CO

2. Keep clicking **Next** until you get to the **Define Output** page (you won't be using any input parameters for this object), and insert a context parameter **Approval** to hold the value later passed to SWF_DEMO_FORMABS_ CREATE.

3. Click **Next** to go to the **Set Configuration** page. Click the [...] icon for the **Approval** parameter to bring up the **Enter Expression** dialog box, and enter the expression "'R'" (including single quote marks).

Although we are entering a very simple expression here, you can browse around the available functions and operators to get a sense of what is possible.

4. Finally, you need to define a result state for a business logic CO, so click the **Add** button, and add a result state **Approved**, giving it an expression of false (no quote marks this time); result states must always return a Boolean value. The result should look something like Figure 4.50.

5. Click **Next**, **Finish and Open,** and then the 🔋 icon (**Activate**) to activate the object.

6. Create a business logic CO for approval in the same way, but this time add an input parameter **Approver** of

type String to contain the user ID of the form's approver. For output parameters, as well as an **Approval** parameter, add **Approver ID** (String) and **Approval Date** (Date) parameters too because FORM-ABSENC objects need to have an approver's ID and the approval date set if the absence is actually approved.

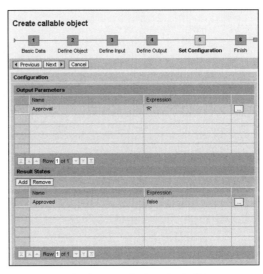

Figure 4.50 Configuring a Business Logic CO

7. Set the expressions for **Approval** to 'A', **Approver ID** to @Approver, and **Approval Date** to NOW(), as shown in Figure 4.51. @Approver copies the value of the **Approver** input parameter to the **Approver ID** output, and NOW() puts the current date into the **Approval Date** output.

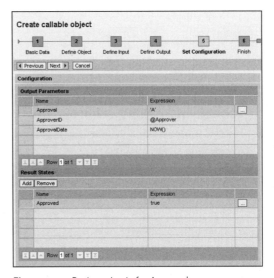

Figure 4.51 Business Logic for Approval

8. After you've finished and activated this object, all the COs for the scenario have been created.

Create Actions from Objects

Now that you've created all the COs, you need to create actions for them (because process blocks are built from actions). For the most part, you'll be creating one action per CO, with the exception being the Get User Information CO where two actions are required: one for the initiator and one for the approver.

1. Go to the Guided Procedures Design Time Gallery, and select **Create Action**, accepting the default language choice.

2. Start with an action for the input form CO, and add a name and description, which might as well be the same as for the CO (see Figure 4.52).

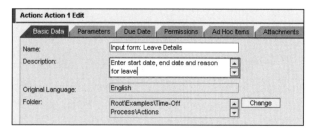

Figure 4.52   Give the Action a Name and Description

3. Click the icon (**Insert**) to assign a CO to this action (see Figure 4.53).

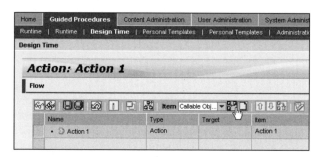

Figure 4.53   Insert CO for Execution

4. Select the CO from the gallery (see Figure 4.54), and click (**Activate**) to activate.

5. Repeat the preceding steps for each of the COs, remembering to create two actions for the Get User Info object: **Get approver info** and **Get initiator info**. That should result in a list of actions that resembles the list in Figure 4.55.

Figure 4.55   Actions for the Absence Approval Process

Compose Process from Actions

Now that the actions are all in place, you're ready to create a simple approval process of just one block. This will consist of the actions with some of their properties set to allow for a decision-based process flow.

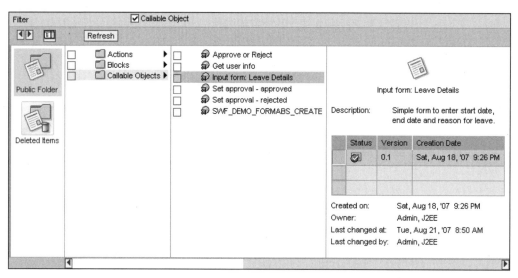

Figure 4.54   Select the CO

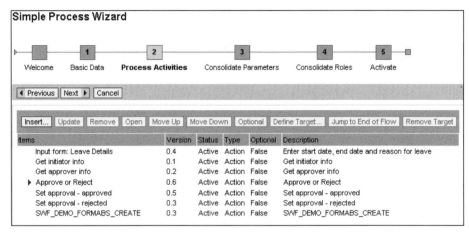

Figure 4.56 List of Actions in the Process

1. Go to the Guided Procedures Design Time, and select **Create Simple Process**. At the **Welcome** screen, click **Next**, then fill in the name and description fields, and make sure the **Block Type** is set to **Sequential** (see Figure 4.56).

2. Add the actions of the process (selecting from existing templates) in the following order (see Figure 4.57):
   - Input form: Leave Details
   - Get initiator info
   - Get approver info
   - Approve or Reject
   - Set approval – approved
   - Set approval – rejected
   - SWF_DEMO_FORMABS_CREATE

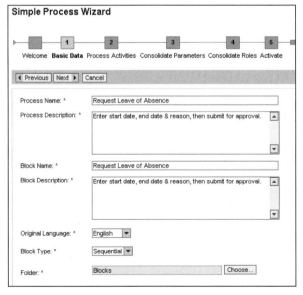

Figure 4.57 First stage of the Create Simple Process Wizard

Consolidating Parameters

Now comes the more complex bit of creating a GP called *parameter consolidation*, which is plumbing the actions together so that the outputs from some actions become the inputs to others.

For example, the **Start Date** from the **Input Form** should be connected to the **Start Date** presented to the **Approve or Reject** approver and should also be passed to SWF_DEMO_FORMABS_CREATE as the Firstday1 element of the Iformdata structure.

1. To do this, click on the checkbox next to each of these fields so that they are highlighted, click the **Map** button, and enter a parameter name to map them to.

2. In Figure 4.58, you can see the parameters being mapped to gStartDate (the FirstDay1 parameter is off the screen). Because the mapped parameters end up as "parameter groups," you should adopt the convention of prefixing the group name with a "g" to make it easier to spot.

> **Tip**
>
> If you need to add any parameters to an existing group, just select the group and the new parameter, and then map them both to the name of the group.

3. The complete list of parameter groups and their consolidated parameters for our absence approval process are shown in Figure 4.59.

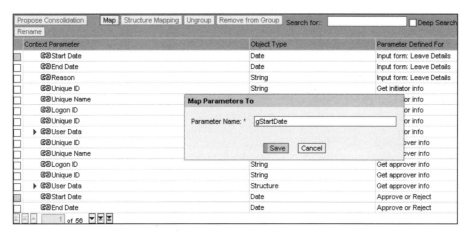

Figure 4.58 Consolidating the Start Date Parameter

Context Parameter	Object Type	Parameter Defined For
▼ gApproval	String	\<Group\>
Approval	String	Set approval - approved
Approval	String	Set approval - rejected
▼ Iformdata	Structure	SWF_DEMO_FORMABS_CREATE
Procstate	String	Iformdata
▼ gStartDate	Date	\<Group\>
Start Date	Date	Input form: Leave Details
Start Date	Date	Approve or Reject
▼ Iformdata	Structure	SWF_DEMO_FORMABS_CREATE
Firstday1	Date	Iformdata
▼ gEndDate	Date	\<Group\>
End Date	Date	Input form: Leave Details
End Date	Date	Approve or Reject
▼ Iformdata	Structure	SWF_DEMO_FORMABS_CREATE
Lastday1	Date	Iformdata
▼ gReason	String	\<Group\>
Reason	String	Input form: Leave Details
Reason	String	Approve or Reject
▼ Iformdata	Structure	SWF_DEMO_FORMABS_CREATE
Reason	String	Iformdata
▼ gFormApproverID	String	\<Group\>
▼ User Data	Structure	Get approver info
Name	String	User Data
Approver	String	Set approval - approved
▼ gFormAbsencApprover	String	\<Group\>
Approver ID	String	Set approval - approved
▼ Iformdata	Structure	SWF_DEMO_FORMABS_CREATE
Approvby	String	Iformdata
▼ gApprovalDate	Date	\<Group\>
Approval Date	Date	Set approval - approved
▼ Iformdata	Structure	SWF_DEMO_FORMABS_CREATE
Approvdate	Date	Iformdata
▼ gUser	String	\<Group\>
▼ User Data	Structure	Get initiator info
Display Name	String	User Data
▼ Iformdata	Structure	SWF_DEMO_FORMABS_CREATE
Name	String	Iformdata
▼ gLoginId	String	\<Group\>
▼ User Data	Structure	Get initiator info
Name	String	User Data
▼ Iformdata	Structure	SWF_DEMO_FORMABS_CREATE
Createdby	String	Iformdata
▼ gApproverLastName	String	\<Group\>
▼ User Data	Structure	Get approver info
Last Name	String	User Data
Approver Last Name	String	Approve or Reject
▼ gApproverFirstName	String	\<Group\>
▼ User Data	Structure	Get approver info
First Name	String	User Data
Approver First Name	String	Approve or Reject

Figure 4.59 Parameter Consolidation for the Absence Approval Process

4. After you've consolidated the parameters, click **Next**, and move on to the **Consolidate Roles** page. You now want to consolidate the list of roles shown into the two roles important for our process: the **Absence Requester** and the **Absence Approver**.

5. Select the roles **Processor of Input form: Leave Details** and **Processor of Get initiator info**, enter **Absence Requester** into the **Consolidate To** field, and click the **Go** button, as shown in Figure 4.60.

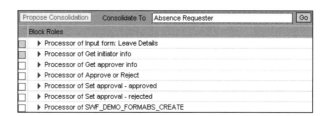

Figure 4.60 Consolidating Absence Requester Roles

6. After you've done the Absence Requester role, select the remaining **Processor of...** roles, and consolidate them to **Absence Approver**. You should end up with roles consolidated as in Figure 4.61.

Block Roles	Type	Items
▼ Absence Requester	G	2
Processor of Input form: Leave Details	U	Input form: Leave Details
Processor of Get initiator info	U	Get initiator info
▼ Absence Approver	G	5
Processor of Get approver info	U	Get approver info
Processor of Approve or Reject	U	Approve or Reject
Processor of Set approval - approved	U	Set approval - approved
Processor of Set approval - rejected	U	Set approval - rejected
Processor of SWF_DEMO_FORMABS_CREATE	U	SWF_DEMO_FORMABS_CREATE

Figure 4.61 Consolidating Roles

7. We're not quite done yet, but the wizard has done all it can to help us, so click **Next**, uncheck the box **Activate the new block and process template**, and click **Finish**.

8. We need to do a bit more role consolidation, so locate the newly created process in the Design Time Gallery (you may need to click the **Refresh** button to see it), and open it up for editing.

9. After the process is opened up, go to the **Built-In Roles** tab, and set each of the three roles to be **Initiator** (see Figure 4.62).

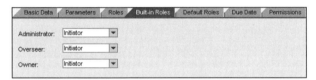

Figure 4.62 Consolidate Built-in Roles to Initiator

10. Click the **Roles** tab, and set the **Absence Requester** to be **Initiator** too, which means that whoever starts the process will be the one filling in the form.

11. Leave **Absence Approver** as **Initiation Defined**, which means that the process initiator will choose who will approve the leave of absence (see Figure 4.63).

A more sophisticated process with a SAP ERP HCM system connected could automatically call the HCM system and make the requester's manager the approver, but that option is left as an exercise for you.

Process Flow Logic

Now is the time to fill in the process flow logic to match the flowchart shown at the start of this section.

1. In the **Process Flow** area of the screen, drill down to the row for the **Approve or Reject** action, then click the icon (**Toggle Single Edit Mode**), and click **Yes** when asked "Do you want to update to inactive version?"

2. Drill down into the action, and set the **Result State Target** for each outcome to the corresponding **Set approval…** action.

3. Go to each of the **Set approval…** actions and set their result state targets to SWF_DEMO_FORMABS_CREATE. You are sending the process down one of two routes — approved or rejected — before converging back at RFC. Figure 4.64 shows how the **Target** settings for the process should look.

Parameter Visibility

The final part of configuring the process is to mark the context parameters visible at process level as nonexposed, so that they are not shown to the initiator of the process.

1. Click on the **Parameters** tab for the process object, uncheck the **Exposed** box for each parameter as shown in Figure 4.65, and click **Save Changes** when you're done.

2. Although you have now created the process, it's worth doing one more thing to make the process much easier to debug. You can add a runtime view that will let you inspect the outputs of each stage of the process, which is essential when you are developing a new process so that you can diagnose any errors.

3. Go to the **Runtime Views** tab, and click the **Add Generic View** button. Choose the **Process Information** view from the list, and then click the **Add** button to see a screen like Figure 4.66.

4. Finally, save your changes, and click ⬆ (**Activate**) to activate the process.

5. After you have your process running as you expect it to, you can go back in and remove the process information view so that your end users don't see debugging information.

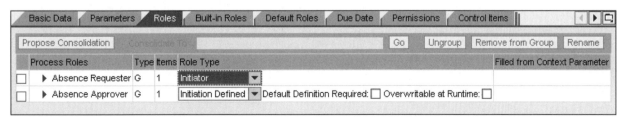

Figure 4.63 Set the Absence Requester to Be the Initiator

Name	Type	Target	Item	Status
▼ Simple absence process	Process		Simple absence process	▨
▼ Simple absence process bloc...	Sequential Block		Simple absence process bloc...	▨
▶ Input form: Leave Details	Action		Input form: Leave Details	▨
▶ Get initiator info	Action		Get initiator info	▨
▶ Get approver info	Action		Get approver info	▨
▼ Approve or Reject	Action		Approve or Reject	▨
▼ Result States				
Input data is rejected	Result State	Set approval - rejected ▼		
Input data is approved	Result State	Set approval - approved ▼		
▼ Set approval - approved	Action		Set approval - approved	▨
▼ Result States				
Approved	Result State	SWF_DEMO_FORMABS_CREATE ▼		
Set approval - approved	Callable Object for Execution		Set approval - approved	▨
▼ Set approval - rejected	Action		Set approval - rejected	▨
▼ Result States				
Approved	Result State	SWF_DEMO_FORMABS_CREATE ▼		
Set approval - rejected	Callable Object for Execution		Set approval - rejected	▨
▶ SWF_DEMO_FORMABS_CREATE	Action		SWF_DEMO_FORMABS_CREATE	▨

Figure 4.64 Setting Result Stage Targets for the Process

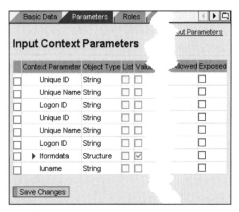

Figure 4.65 Marking Parameters as Not Exposed

Testing the Guided Procedure

To test this process, you'll need two users, each with the GP User portal role. One user will create an absence request and will get the other user to approve it.

Create Absence Request

Start the absence request process as follows:

1. Log in to the portal as the absence requester, go to the **Guided Procedures • Runtime** menu, and click on the link **Initiate a New Process** (see Figure 4.67).

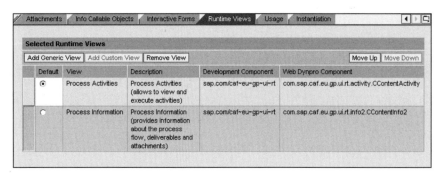

Figure 4.66 Adding the Process Information Runtime View

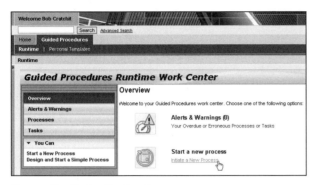

Figure 4.67   Testing the New Process

2. Navigate the Guided Procedures folders to find and select the process, and then click **Next** (see Figure 4.68).

3. Make sure **Single Instantiation** is selected, then search for the appropriate approver, and click the **Add** button to assign the approver to the **Absence Approver** role (see Figure 4.69).

4. Click the **Next** button, fill in the process name, and click **Initiate** to start the process (see Figure 4.70). Because the process maps the initiator to be the form creator, you are taken straight to the input form, which is the first step of the process (see Figure 4.71).

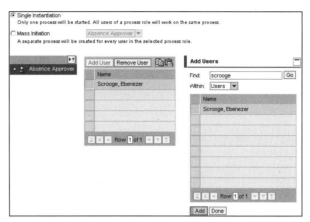

Figure 4.69   Select the Approver

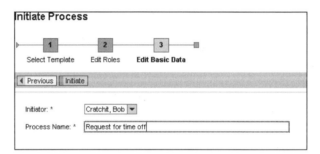

Figure 4.70   Initiate the Process

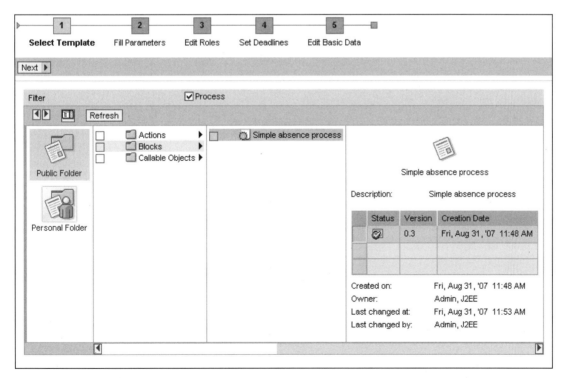

Figure 4.68   Selecting the Process to Start

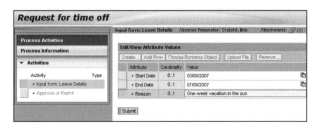

Figure 4.71   Absence Details Input Form

5. Fill in the absence details, and then click the **Submit** button. You will then see a message saying that the "Action is ready for processing by another user or role." The input form activity will have a tick indicating completion, and the **Approve** or **Reject** activity will be highlighted. A status bar at the top of the screen should inform you that this activity is assigned to the **Absence Approver** (see Figure 4.72).

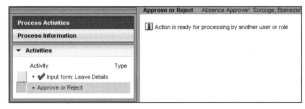

Figure 4.72   Process Status after Submitting Form

Approve Absence

Now it's time to log into the portal as the approver.

1. Go to the **Guided Procedures • Runtime** menu in the **Work Center's Overview** section, and you should see **Tasks that require my action (1)**, indicating that there is a task for you. Click on the related link **Tasks Where Action is Required to Continue Process Flow,** and you should be taken to a list of open tasks as shown in Figure 4.73.

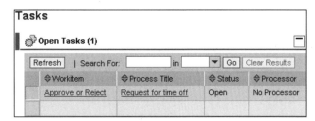

Figure 4.73   GP Tasks for Processing

2. Click on the work item's title, and you will be taken to the **Approve or Reject** processing screen, which will show you the details of the absence request and allow

you to enter a comment (which, in this version of the process, is ignored). You can see this in Figure 4.74.

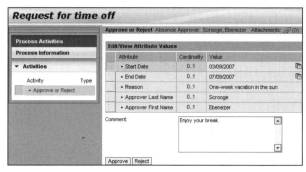

Figure 4.74   Approval Action for Absence Request

3. Click the **Approve** button to approve the request. You will see that an email notification has been sent to the absence requester, and the process has moved to the action **Set approval – approved**, as expected (see Figure 4.75).

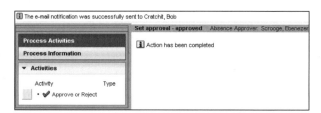

Figure 4.75   Approve or Reject Action Completed

If you now go and check the absence requester's email inbox, you should see an email generated by the **Leave Approval** email template you created in "Create Email Templates for Approval and Rejection" in Section 4.3 (see Figure 4.76).

Figure 4.76   Email Generated After a Successful Approval

You can also click on the **Process Information** section of the process display at this point to see the output parameters of the steps your user has been involved in (or all of the steps in the process if you are the process administra-

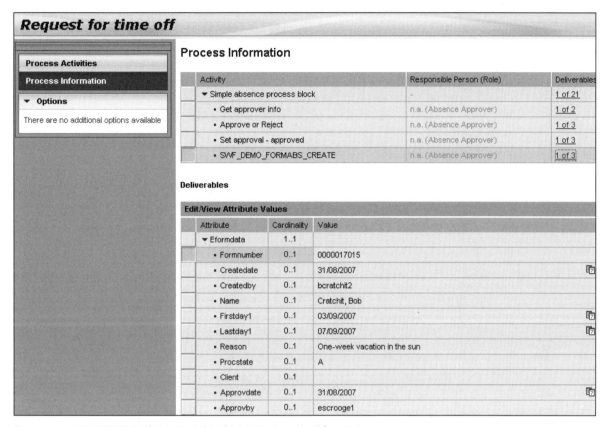

Figure 4.77   FORMABSENC Object Created in the SAP Business Workflow System

tor — the initiator in this case). Figure 4.77 shows the absence approver looking at the output of the SWF_DEMO_ FORMABS_CREATE action, which shows the details of the FORMABSENC object created in the SAP Business Workflow system as a result of the process.

You should now have an idea of what you can do with GPs. Although the example here is quite simple, it shows how to create a form-driven approval process that puts its results into a back end SAP Business Workflow system. To get really interesting, you could look at a GP that gets started when a user emails a completed Adobe form to the system, but that's beyond the scope of this book.

Integrating Guided Procedures with UWL

To make GP tasks appear in UWL, you need to register the GP system as a provider of UWL tasks, in a similar way to how you registered an SAP Business Workflow system in Chapter 2. A brief description follows; you can find full details in the SAP Help Portal at **Developing, Configuring, and Adapting Applications • Creating Composite Applications • CAF-GP: Configuration Guide • Parameter Config-**

uration • **Configuring Guided Procedures with the Universal Worklist**.

To start with, you need to create a system entry in the portal for accessing Web Services on the GP system (usually, the portal itself).

1. Navigate to **System Administration • System Configuration • System Landscape,** and create a **New • System (from PAR).**

2. Select the portal archive com.sap.portal.systems.webservices from the list, and accept the default portal component of webservice_system.

3. Give the system a name and ID, and then open the system for editing when asked.

4. Choose the **Web Services** property category, and for the **WSDL URL,** enter the address of the portal (without the /irj path), for example, *http://portal.fortybeans.com:50000.*

5. Save this entry, and then give the system an alias, for example, "GP_Local", by going to the **System Aliases** display.

Inbox							☰

Tasks (1 / 1)   Alerts   Notifications   Tracking   ◀ ▶ ▣

Show: New and In Progress Tasks (1 / 1) ▼ Select a Subview... ▼ All ▼ Create Task Show Filters Hide Preview ≣

	Subject ⇕	!	From ⇕	Sent ⇕	Priority ⇕	📎	Due ⇕	Status ⇕
	Approve or Reject		**Cratchit, Bob**	**Today**	**Normal**			**New**

Figure 4.78   Guided Procedure Task in UWL

6. Now that the system has been created and given an alias, navigate to **System Administration • System Con-figuration • Universal Worklist & Workflow • Universal Worklist – Administration,** and click on the **New** button.

7. Enter the system alias you just created, and set the **Connector Type** to GuidedProceduresConnector.

That's all there is to it. If you log in to the portal as the approver after someone submits a leave request, you will now see an item in UWL, as shown in Figure 4.78 (the subject of the item is taken from the action name). Clicking on the item launches the GP action in just the same way as if you had done it from the GP runtime screen.

4.4   Third-Party Workflow

With some Java programming skill and the UWL API, you can write your own connector for UWL. Your users will be able to see work items and notifications from other systems, such as their Microsoft Outlook Tasks, RSS feeds, or SAP Office emails. SAP has used the API to provide a proof of concept for retrieving SAP Office emails; see the reference "Connecting SAP Office Mail to the Universal Worklist" in Table B.3 in Appendix B.

SAP's documentation and training material in this area is very good, so this section will only skim the surface to give you an idea of what's involved with writing your own connector. For full details, see the reference "Universal Worklist API" in Table B.3 in Appendix B as well.

In brief, there are two main aspects that you need for your own UWL connector:

▶ **Item provider**
  How to get the items.

▶ **Action handler**
  What to do when a user clicks a button.

In the following example, you'll see a simple item provider that constructs a bug from an external bug-tracking system, Bugzilla, and the simplest possible action handler, which just launches the Bugzilla web application with the selected bug loaded up. You can modify and extend this example to create a connector of your own — the idea here is to show you just how simple it is to get going.

Getting Started

To start building your third-party UWL connector, follow these steps:

1. Launch the SAP NetWeaver Developer Studio (NWDS), select **File • New Project...,** and choose the **UWL Custom Connector Project** from the **Universal Worklist (UWL)** section, as shown in Figure 4.79.

2. Give the new project a name (e.g., "BugzillaUWLConnector") and a supported item type for use in the UWL configuration file (e.g., uwl.task.mybug), and click **Finish** (see Figure 4.80).

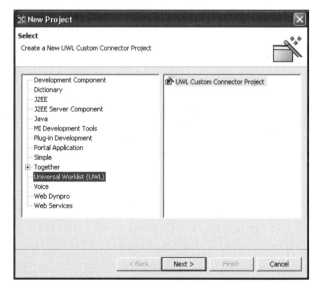

Figure 4.79   Creating a Third-Party UWL Connector in NWDS

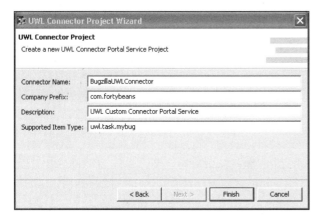

Figure 4.80   Setting the Properties for the Project Wizard

3. This creates a project with all of the code ready to go. All you need to do is fill in the code for your specific scenario. To help you further, there are @TODO comments in the code that show up in the NWDS tasks view (see Figure 4.81) and guide you through the process step-by-step. Even better, as you'll see next, a minimal connector only requires you to complete item TODO 4 and then either item 6 or item 7.

Figure 4.81   Auto-Generated Tasks in the UWL Connector Code

4. The project wizard also creates a sample UWL configuration file for your new connector in `dist/PORTAL-INF/`, which gets uploaded into the portal as soon as you deploy your connector.

Getting Items from the Back End

The first thing to do is to write the code that fetches tasks from another system.

1. You need to get a set of work items for the requesting user from the back end system by implementing the body of the `getItems()` method (item TODO 4). You can get the current user ID by calling `context.getUserId()`, and the system name is passed in as a parameter, which gives you all you need to look up the system in the Portal System Landscape, perform any user

mapping, make a connection using an appropriate protocol, and retrieve the items.

2. The code shown in Listing 4.3 is much simpler; it just creates an item from scratch and returns an item collection based on the one item. The code shown is the same as generated by the wizard, except for the sections in bold.

```
public ConnectorResult getItems(
    UWLContext context,
    String itemType,
    ConnectorFilter connectorFilter,
    String system)
    throws ConnectorException {

    ConnectorResult result = null;
    List items = null;
    /**
     * @TODO 4: Implement getItems
     * Connect with your Item Provider and fetch
     * the items for the itemType. Map the items
     * from the item Provider to UWL Items.
     */
    Item item1 = new Item(
        BugzillaUWLConnector.CONNECTOR_ID,
        system,                   // systemID
        "1",                      // externalID
        context.getUserId(),      // userID
        -1,                       // attachmentCount
        new Date(),               // createdDate
        "bugzilla",               // creatorID
        null,                     // dueDate
        null,                     // externalObjectID
        myItemTypes[0],           // externalType
        myItemTypes[0],           // itemType
        PriorityEnum.LOW,         // priority
        StatusEnum.NEW,           // status
        "Bug 1");                 // subject

    item1.setDescription(
        "Spelling mistake on login screen");
```

Listing 4.3   Toy Implementation of getItems()

```
item1.setExecutionUrl(
  "http://bugzilla.fortybeans.com/"
  + "show_bug.cgi?id="
  + item1.getExternalId());

Attribute att1 = Attribute.createAttribute(
  "severity", "minor");

item1.addAttribute(att1);

// Add items to list
items = new ArrayList();
items.add(item1);

ProviderStatus  status = new
    ProviderStatus(true,system,
    BugzillaUWLConnector.CONNECTOR_ID);
/**
 * @TODO 5: Decide if DeltaResult or Snapshot
 *   result should be created.
 */
result = ConnectorResult.createSnapshotResult
(
    new ItemCollection(items),status);

  return result;
}
```

Listing 4.3   Toy Implementation of getItems() (cont.)

Note how `Attribute.createAttribute()` and `item1.addAttribute()` are used to create and add a custom attribute to the item.

3. This attribute is now available for display in UWL using the same customizations as shown in Chapters 2 and 3.

Configuring Item Display

In fact, the next task is to modify the XML configuration file created by the wizard to show the new severity attribute in the custom view for the new item.

1. Add a new `DisplayAttribute` to the view.
2. Add `severity` to the list of columns in the view's `columnOrder` attribute (see Listing 4.4).

```xml
<View name="BugzillaUWLConnectorView" width="98%"
  supportedItemTypes="uwl.task.mybugs"
  columnOrder="detailIcon,subject,severity,
    creatorId,createdDate,statusIcon,status"
  sortby="creatorId:ascend, createdDate:descend"
  emphasizedItems="new"
  selectionMode="MULTISELECT"
  tableDesign="STANDARD"
  visibleRowCount="10"
  headerVisible="yes"
  tableNavigationFooterVisible="yes"
  tableNavigationType="CUSTOMNAV"
  actionRef="">
<Descriptions default="Bugs assigned to me"/>
<DisplayAttributes>
  <DisplayAttribute
    name="createdDate" type="datetime"
    width="" sortable="yes" format="medium"
    referenceBundle="sent_date"
    hAlign="LEFT" vAlign="BASELINE"
    maxTextWidth="0" headerVisible="yes"/>
  <DisplayAttribute
    name="severity" type="string" />
</DisplayAttributes>
<Actions>
  <Action reference="complete" />
</Actions>
</View>
```

Listing 4.4   XML Configuration File for the Connector

3. Finally, change the default description of "This is a sample view generated by the UWL Connector Wizard for your Item Type" to the more meaningful "Bugs assigned to me."

Handling Actions

Now that the items have been fetched and displayed, it's time to act on them.

1. For our simple example, we just want to launch the Bugzilla application and let the user do all the processing there.

2. Because the item's `executionUrl` property was already set in `getItems()`, all that remains is to implement `getUrl()` to return that property and to tell `isLauncher()` to return `true` so that the application is

launched instead of the action being processed by UWL (see Listing 4.5).

```
public String getUrl(UWLContext context,
  Item item, Action action, Map properties)
  throws UWLException {
  /**
   * @TODO 6: Decide if getUrl needs to be
   *    implemented. Check UWL API javadoc
   */
  return item.getExecutionUrl();
}


public boolean isLauncher() {
  return true;
}
```

Listing 4.5 Item Handler for Launching a Web Page with No UWL Interaction

3. If the user's action was something like selecting an **Approve** or **Reject** button, then there may be no need to launch the third-party application in a browser window. The action might instead be done using some kind of RFC or Web Service invocation. In this case, isLauncher() should be set to return false, and the performAction() method should be implemented to make the call to the third-party application back end.

Deploying and Testing

To deploy your new UWL connector to the portal, follow these steps:

1. Export the project as a PAR file, and deploy it using the NWDS (using the **Quick PAR Upload** option), or deploy the PAR file through the portal (via **System Administration • Support • Portal Runtime • Administration Console**). The XML configuration file from the PAR file will be automatically uploaded as a UWL configuration.
2. To configure the usage of the connection, first create a System Landscape entry for your back end system, and give it an alias. Then create a new UWL system just like

you did in Chapter 2 (**System Administration • System Configuration • Universal Worklist & Workflow • Universal Worklist – Administration**), give it the alias of the system you created, and select your new connector from the dropdown list (see Figure 4.82).

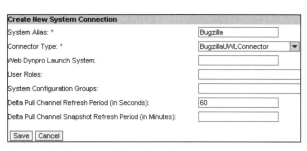

Figure 4.82 Configure UWL with a New Connector

3. That's really all there is to it. You can now log in as one of your users, and you should see a bug from Bugzilla in the UWL.
4. Click on the **Complete** button, and a new window should launch with the relevant bug loaded up and ready to go, as shown in Figure 4.83.

4.5   Summary

In this chapter, you learned that the UWL can be used for much more than processing work items from SAP Business Workflow systems. You saw how simple it is for users to set up and track one-off tasks and processes using ad-hoc workflow, and you saw the publishing workflow from the portal's Knowledge Management component, from which tasks and notifications appear in the UWL.

Next you discovered how a Business Process Expert with no SAP Business Workflow knowledge can create repeatable business processes in the portal using Guided Procedures. If all that wasn't enough, in the final part of the chapter you learned how to write your own connectors in Java to enable your users to see tasks from non-SAP workflow systems in the UWL.

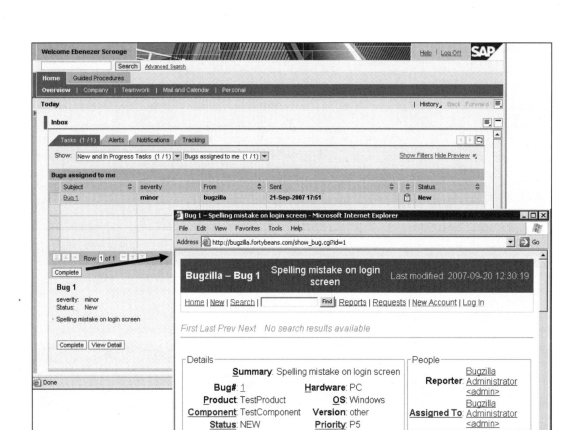

Figure 4.83   Third-Party Workflow System Launched from Item View in UWL

5 UWL Behind the Scenes

In the other chapters of this book, you have seen how to set up and work with UWL as a portal administrator. This chapter takes you around the back and shows you the effects of your configuration so that when things go wrong, you have an idea why and what you should do about it.

▶ Section 5.1 shows you basic troubleshooting techniques for when UWL behavior is not what you expect. UWL support information will help you check that your carefully crafted XML configuration is actually being used; bumping up the detail written to the J2EE logs and looking at what gets written to them will help you resolve connection issues.

▶ Section 5.2 looks at performance, which is more likely to be useful in a production support situation when users are getting the right information but they are having to wait too long to get it; sometimes the information is correct but out of date. You will learn how to configure UWL for the best combination of performance and accuracy.

▶ Section 5.3 goes deep and looks at the sequence of Remote Function Calls (RFCs) that get made from the portal to the back end SAP Business Workflow system. This can be very useful for workflow troubleshooting by allowing you to place breakpoints in the relevant function modules so you can trace through exactly what is happening in the backend in response to user actions in the UWL front end.

▶ Section 5.4 tackles the realization that no system is perfect by looking at some of the limitations of UWL and web-based SAP Business Workflow. There are not many limitations, but it's very important to know what they are so that you can set the right expectations and make the appropriate trade-offs when designing a UWL-based business task management system.

5.1 Troubleshooting UWL

In this section, you'll find out about the diagnostic information available in UWL, part of which can be turned on in the UWL iView, and part of which is visible in the SAP NetWeaver Java log files.

UWL Support Information

You can get a lot of useful information about individual work items by going into the PCD (**Content Administration • Portal Content**) and setting the UWL iView's **Display UWL Support Information** property to **Yes**. After you do this, selecting any item in the worklist will lead to a collection of information panes being shown at the bottom of the screen:

▶ The first pane (see Figure 5.1) shows details of the currently logged-on user and a summary of some of the iView attributes controlling the look and feel of UWL.

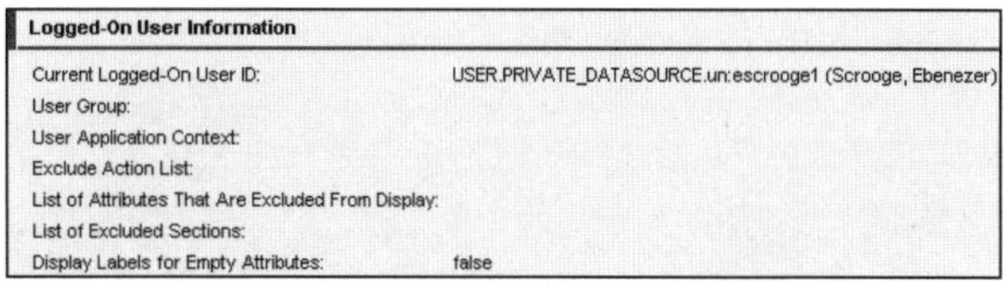

Logged-On User Information	
Current Logged-On User ID:	USER.PRIVATE_DATASOURCE.un:escrooge1 (Scrooge, Ebenezer)
User Group:	
User Application Context:	
Exclude Action List:	
List of Attributes That Are Excluded From Display:	
List of Excluded Sections:	
Display Labels for Empty Attributes:	false

Figure 5.1 Logged-On User and UWL iView Attributes

▶ The second pane (see Figure 5.2) shows details of the current item's view. Effectively, this is telling you about the <View> section of the XML configuration file that is being used.

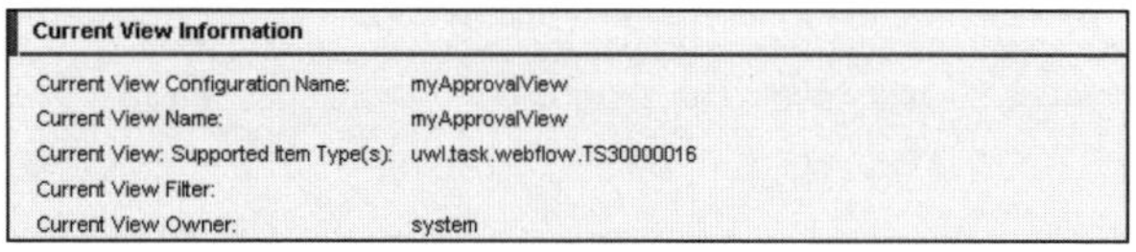

Current View Information	
Current View Configuration Name:	myApprovalView
Current View Name:	myApprovalView
Current View: Supported Item Type(s):	uwl.task.webflow.TS30000016
Current View Filter:	
Current View Owner:	system

Figure 5.2 Current View Information

▶ The third pane (see Figure 5.3) shows the current navigation node being used, which corresponds to the `<NavigationNode>` element being used from the XML configuration file.

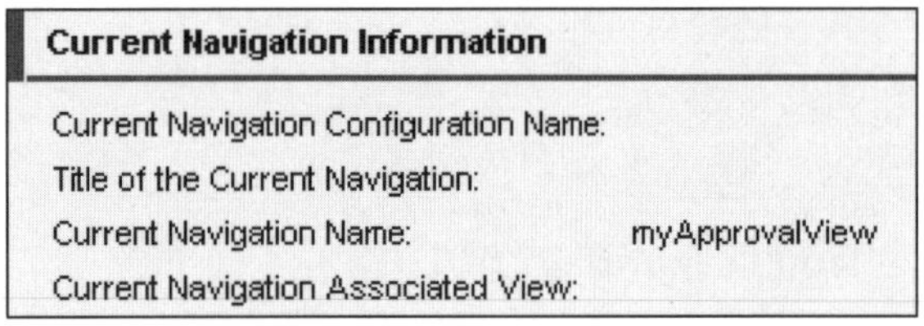

Current Navigation Information

Current Navigation Configuration Name:
Title of the Current Navigation:
Current Navigation Name: myApprovalView
Current Navigation Associated View:

Figure 5.3   Current Navigation Information

▶ The fourth and final pane (see Figure 5.4) is perhaps the most useful for troubleshooting purposes. It shows the item type (which is pattern-matched when UWL looks for the relevant XML configuration entry), the SAP Business Workflow task type of the current item, and the external item ID (which is the work item ID in SAP Business Workflow). The list of supported attributes can help to tell you how successful you are when defining UWL custom attributes.

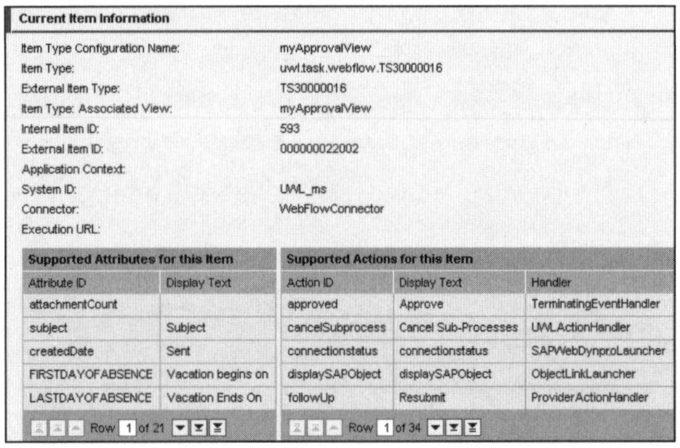

Current Item Information

Item Type Configuration Name:	myApprovalView
Item Type:	uwl.task.webflow.TS30000016
External Item Type:	TS30000016
Item Type: Associated View:	myApprovalView
Internal Item ID:	593
External Item ID:	000000022002
Application Context:	
System ID:	UWL_ms
Connector:	WebFlowConnector
Execution URL:	

Supported Attributes for this Item		Supported Actions for this Item		
Attribute ID	Display Text	Action ID	Display Text	Handler
attachmentCount		approved	Approve	TerminatingEventHandler
subject	Subject	cancelSubprocess	Cancel Sub-Processes	UWLActionHandler
createdDate	Sent	connectionstatus	connectionstatus	SAPWebDynproLauncher
FIRSTDAYOFABSENCE	Vacation begins on	displaySAPObject	displaySAPObject	ObjectLinkLauncher
LASTDAYOFABSENCE	Vacation Ends On	followUp	Resubmit	ProviderActionHandler

Figure 5.4   Current Item Information

UWL Logs

When you get confusing or terse error messages from the portal, the best place to look for more detail is in the SAP NetWeaver log files. The Standalone Log Viewer is the best tool to use for this, and you can get a copy of it from the SAP NetWeaver server for running on a client PC (being Java-based, the log viewer is a cross-platform piece of software). If you need more detail in the logs, use the Log Configurator to specify how much detail to show for each area of portal functionality.

Portal Log Viewer

The log viewer (see Figure 5.5) is available at `/usr/sap/<SID>/.../j2ee/admin/logviewer-standalone`; just copy this folder to your local machine, and run `logviewer.bat` (assuming you are running Windows) or `logviewer.sh` (for UNIX-based operating systems). You will need to create a connection to the SAP NetWeaver Java server on the P4 port; this is the web port number plus 4, so if you normally access the portal using *http://portal.fortybeans.com:50000/irj*, then the log viewer connection will be to `portal.fortybeans.com` on port `50004`.

You can also view the same logs through your web browser using the SAP NetWeaver Administrator. This is not quite so easy to use but may be easier for you to access on a project where security concerns may prevent you from accessing anything other than the standard web ports. To access the web interface, do the following:

1. In your browser, go to *http://portal.fortybeans.com:50000/nwa* (in other words, the usual portal URL but replacing */irj* with */nwa*).
2. Navigate to **System Management • Monitoring • Logs and Traces**.
3. At the top of the screen next to **Show,** select **Predefined View** and **Expert**.
4. At the label **Display log file,** choose the log file to show from the dropdown list

Some of the most useful logs for UWL purposes are shown in Table 5.1.

Log File	Location	Purpose
defaultTrace.trc	`<instance>/j2ee/cluster/serverx/log`	This is the general-purpose log file for the portal.
uwl_default-Log.log	`<instance>/j2ee/cluster/serverx/log/applications/sap.com/uwl`	This is the specific log file for UWL.
workflow.%g.log	`<instance>/j2ee/cluster/serverx/log/applications/workflow`	This is the log file for portal-based workflow.

Table 5.1   UWL Log File Locations

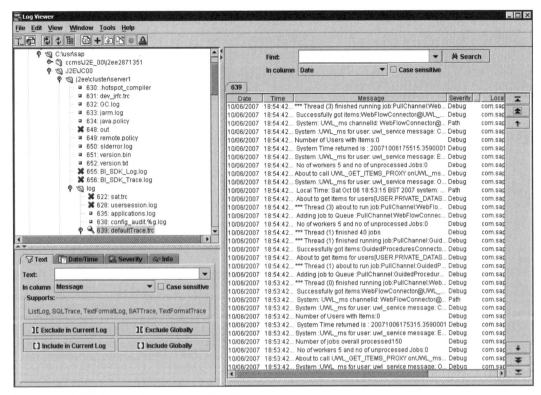

Figure 5.5   SAP NetWeaver Java Standalone Log Viewer

Your first port of call for debugging anything in the portal should always be `defaultTrace.trc`, which will contain the information you are looking for 90% of the time. If you don't have any luck there, then either go to one of the more specialized log files, such as the workflow log shown in the web interface in Figure 5.6, or configure the logs to show more information, as described next.

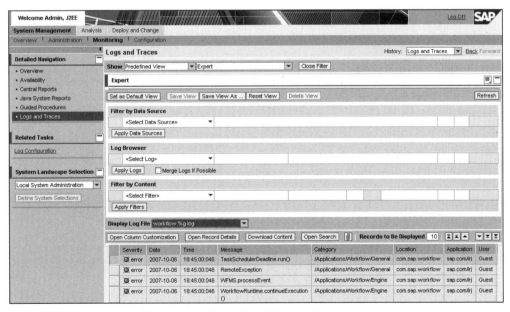

Figure 5.6   Viewing Logs in a Web Browser Using SAP NetWeaver Administrator

Portal Log Configurator

To get more information in the logs, particularly when you're trying to debug connection issues, you will need to use the Log Configurator in Visual Administrator. If you don't have a local copy of Visual Administrator, then (like the Log Viewer), you can copy the cross-platform Java application from the SAP NetWeaver Application Server.

1. Copy the files from */usr/sap/<SID>/.../j2ee/admin* to your local machine, and run `go.bat` (Windows) or `go.sh` (UNIX) to launch the Visual Administrator.
2. Navigate to **Server • Services • Log Configurator**.
3. Drill down by **Categories** (see Figure 5.7) and/or **Locations** (see Figure 5.8).
4. Set the preferred logging levels.

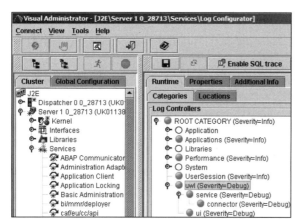

Figure 5.7   Log Configurator Categories for UWL

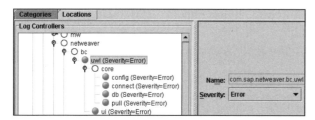

Figure 5.8   Log Configurator Locations for UWL

5. Some useful logging categories include the following:
   ▶ `/uwl` and subcategories
   ▶ `/Applications/CAFCore_GP` for GPs
   ▶ `/Applications/Workflow` subcategories

Some useful logging locations include the following:
▶ `com.fortybeans.uwl` and sublocations for third-party UWL connectors, assuming you defined the company prefix as "com.fortybeans"

▶ `com.sap.caf.core.gp` for GPs
▶ `com.sap.caf.eu.gp` for GPs
▶ `com.sap.mbs.ca.RIMAuthentication` for the Black-Berry JAAS login module
▶ `com.sap.netweaver.bc.uwl` and sublocations for UWL
▶ `com.sap.portal.JCOClientPool` for RFC connection pooling issues
▶ `com.sap.portal.connectors` and sublocations for debugging connection issues, especially when doing connection tests with Portal System Landscape entries
▶ `com.sap.workflow` and sublocations for portal-based workflow (i.e., collaboration tasks)

In each case, when using the Log Configurator, you should increase the detail one level at a time until you see information of use to you, and you should reduce the logging level back to its original value as soon as you have finished so that you avoid filling up the disk or database with log files.

5.2   UWL Performance Tuning

This section looks at how to get the best performance from your UWL deployment. First of all, you'll find out about a recent development, the delta-pull mechanism for getting work items from a SAP Business Workflow system, which leads to a great improvement in performance. Next, you'll see how to restrict from which systems each user gets work items according to their roles, which reduces the number of unnecessary calls over the network. Finally, you'll see the parameters you can tune to get that final few percent of performance out of your system.

Delta-Pull Mechanism

In normal operation, UWL calls the SAP Business Workflow system for each user that is logged into the portal. This can cause performance problems, especially at the start of the day when lots of users are logging in within a short period of time, causing a large number of simultaneous RFC connections to the back end. The delta-pull mechanism avoids this by setting up two batch jobs on the back end, one to get all items for all users (run once per day) and another to get changes to users' worklists (run every few minutes).

The portal contacts the back end periodically to retrieve these items on behalf of all users, usually leading to a much smaller and more predictable performance impact. A guide to setting this up is provided next. The detailed SAP documentation is in the SAP Help Portal at **Business Task Management • Universal Worklist Configuration • Optional Configuration • Enabling Delta Pull Mechanism**.

Enabling Delta-Pull in the SAP Business Workflow System
When you register a SAP Business Workflow system with UWL, the portal calls the function module UWL_CREATE_SERVICE_USER, which causes the back end system to create the communications user UWL_SERVICE with the following roles:

▶ SAP_BC_BMT_WFM_UWL_END_USER

▶ SAP_BC_UWL_END_USER

▶ SAP_BC_UWL_SERVICE

If for any reason your back end system does not have this user, or the user has different roles, then you should correct this situation manually using transaction SU01 in the back end system. Note that if Central User Administration (CUA) is in place, then you will need to do this on the CUA Master client.

The first time you register the system, you will see a message like "The back end of system XX is not configured for optimized delta pull," which just means that the batch jobs have not yet been set up.

Setting Up the Background Jobs
You need to schedule two batch jobs to run (using transaction SA38 with the **Background** option), one for the full scan and one for the delta scan. In each case, the job should run the same program, RSWNUWLSEL. For the full scan, you will have to create a variant for **FULL** mode, and for the delta scan, you will have to create a variant for **DELTA** mode. These variants can be created using transaction SE38, executing RSWNUWLSEL, and then pressing [Ctrl]+[S] to save a variant after you have selected the relevant option.

Figure 5.9 shows the initial screen with **DELTA Filter** mode selected just before saving the variant.

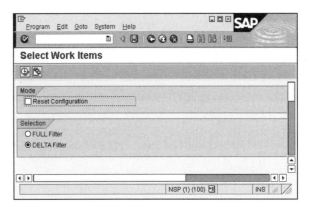

Figure 5.9 Report RSWNUWLSEL for Delta-Pull

You should schedule the full scan to run once per day and the delta scan to run once every minute or so.

Configuring Delta-Pull in the Portal
Now that the back end is set up, you need to adjust the settings in the portal.

1. Navigate to **System Administration • System Configuration • Universal Worklist & Workflow • Universal Worklist – Administration**.

2. Select the UWL system for the SAP Business Workflow back end.

3. Click the **Edit** button.

4. Set the values for **Delta Pull Channel Refresh Period** and **Snapshot Refresh Period** to the same frequency as the jobs on the back end; 1440 minutes is one day (see Figure 5.10).

5. Click **Save**.

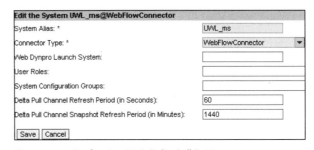

Figure 5.10 Configuring UWL Delta-Pull Settings

Roles and System Configuration Groups

Another way of improving UWL performance is to recognize that users have different roles, and not all roles access all systems. For example, a purchasing manager will require access to an SAP SRM system, but an HR administrator may not.

5 UWL Behind the Scenes

Filtering Access by Role

The User Roles entry in the UWL system configuration (**System Administration • System Configuration • Universal Worklist & Workflow • Universal Worklist – Administration**) allows you to specify the roles that have access to each system. When users see UWL in their portals, only the systems corresponding to their roles are checked for work items. This has the added advantage that users are not confused by connection error messages for back end systems where they do not have an account.

You specify the allowable roles for each system using the role's ID in the Portal Content Directory (PCD), including any prefix but without the PCD folder path. For example, a role "UWL Book" whose full PCD URL is `pcd:portal_content/UWL_Book/com.fortybeans.UWL_book` would be listed in the UWL roles list as just `com.fortybeans.UWL_book`. You can specify several roles for a system as a list of role IDs separated by semicolons (;).

Filtering Access by System Configuration Group

Another way of achieving the same thing is to use system configuration groups. This is an older method, and SAP now recommends that you use the roles method described previously. In case you are dealing with an older system, however, here is how system configuration groups work:

▶ You specify a comma- or semicolon-separated list of strings for each UWL system's **System Configuration Groups** property.

▶ You create a version of the UWL iView for each group, setting the **System Configuration Group** property to one of the values.

▶ You assign each iView to the roles relevant for that group of systems.

As an example, suppose that most of your users use the portal just for Knowledge Management (KM) and collaboration. A smaller number of users also use SAP ERP functionality, and only these users have accounts on the SAP ERP system. Here's how to set things up, first the UWL configuration and then the iViews:

1. In the Universal Worklist Administration screen (**System Administration • System Configuration • Universal Worklist & Workflow • Universal Worklist – Administration**), for the SAP ERP system, add "SAP_ERP" as a

System Configuration Groups entry as shown in Figure 5.11. This tells the portal to connect to this system only from a UWL iView configured for the group SAP_ERP.

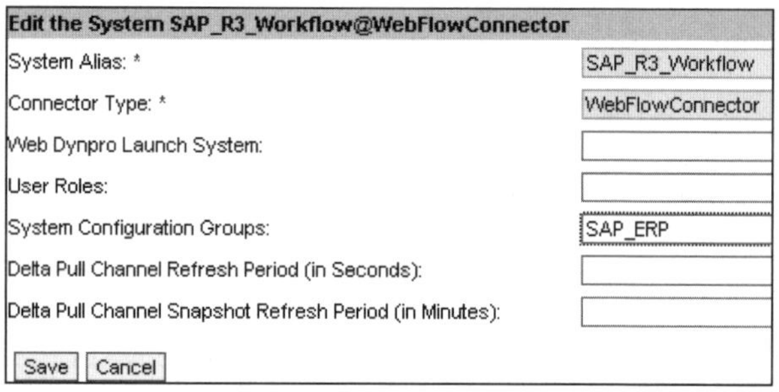

Figure 5.11 Setting the System Configuration Group for a SAP ERP UWL System Entry

2. For the other UWL system entries (**AdHocSystem**, **ActionInbox**, etc.), set their **System Configuration Groups** entries to "KMuser,SAP_ERP" to indicate that they can be accessed from both UWL iViews (see Figure 5.12).

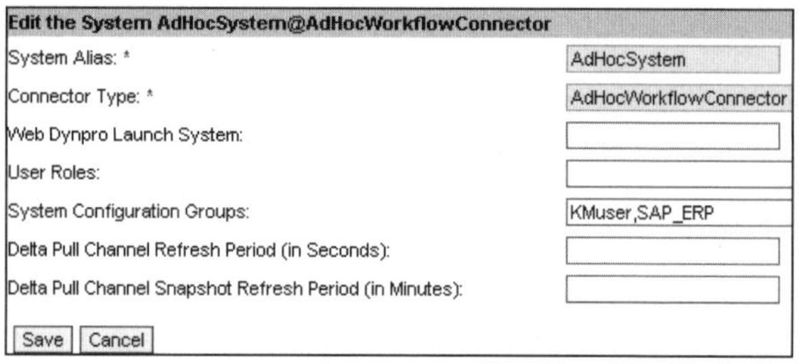

Figure 5.12 Setting the System Configuration Group for a Portal-Only UWL System Entry

3. Navigate to **Content Administration • Portal Content**, and make a delta-linked copy of the UWL iView, calling it "Universal Worklist (ERP)."

4. Open the original UWL iView that you copied. In the **Navigation** section, set the **Merge ID** property to "UWL", and in the **UWL** section, set the **System Configuration Group** property to "KMuser" (see Figure 5.13).

5. Open the new delta-linked copy of the UWL iView. In the **Navigation** section, set the **Merge Priority** property to "50", and in the **UWL** section, set the **System Configuration Group** property to "SAP_ERP" as shown in Figure 5.14.

Figure 5.13 Setting the System Configuration Group on the UWL iView Available to All Users

Figure 5.14 Setting the System Configuration Group Entry on the UWL iView Visible Only to SAP ERP Users

The idea behind setting the **Merge ID** and **Merge Priority** values on the two versions of the iView is that you can assign the first version of the iView, Universal Worklist, to all of your users; for those ERP users who also get assigned the new Universal Worklist (ERP) iView, the new iView will take the place of ("merge over") the original iView in their portal menus. This is easier than trying to come up with two roles that contain mutually exclusive sets of users.

As you can see, using system configuration groups is a more complex approach than specifying user roles because it relies on you creating lots of UWL iViews and assigning them correctly. The roles-based approach is a far simpler way of getting the same performance gain because you only need to use one instance of the UWL iView.

From a wider perspective, the configuration explained in this section also adds an analysis task to your portal implementation: You need to produce a catalogue of all your roles, and for each role, you need to figure out which systems you want work items from. The results of this analysis will enable you to assign the necessary roles for each system in the UWL configuration to ensure the best performance.

Execution Mode, Caching, and Pooling

By default, when a user clicks on an item in UWL, the action is executed without checking if the item is still valid, which leads to a faster response time. However, sometimes accuracy is more important; for example, if an item is waiting for approval by several possible agents, then you don't want the item to be approved by one person and rejected by another. Even if the system protects against multiple decisions, you still don't want to mislead the user with confusing error messages that might give them the (incorrect) impression of an unstable system.

To resolve this issue at the expense of some responsiveness, you should set UWL to run in its **Pessimistic** execution mode instead of the default **Optimistic** mode.

1. Navigate to **System Administration • System Configuration • Universal Worklist & Workflow • Universal Worklist – Administration**.
2. Expand the section **Optional Universal Worklist Service Configuration** by clicking on the **Expand Tray** icon.
3. Click the **Edit** button.
4. Set the **Default Execution Mode** to **Pessimistic** (see Figure 5.15).
5. Click the **Save** button.

Figure 5.15 Changing to Pessimistic Execution Mode

While you are checking out this optional configuration section, you will notice that you can also tweak the following performance-related values:

▶ Cache validity period (in minutes; ignored when using delta-pull)
▶ Number of threads used for the UWL connection pool
▶ How long to wait for items
▶ Number of users for each pull channel

In most cases, you should be able to leave these options set to the default values. If you are dealing with a very heavily loaded system, it may be worth increasing the values (50 % at a time, one at a time) to see if that helps with performance.

5.3   How UWL Talks to SAP Business Workflow

In this section, you'll see which RFCs are called in a SAP Business Workflow system when various actions are carried out in the portal. The main point is that if you have a problem where the information in the SAP NetWeaver Java logs is not enough, you can place HTTP breakpoints in the relevant function modules and trace through what is happening on the back end system. As well as the RFCs mentioned here, there is a full list of useful UWL and SAP_WAPI function modules in Appendix B (see Table B.8). The best way to get more information on each of the function modules is to run transaction SE37 on the SAP Business Workflow system, and enter the name of the function module. This will allow you to see the import/export parameters, the code itself, and occasionally a small amount of documentation.

If you want to trace the RFC calls being made for your particular scenario, you should run transaction ST05 and enable an RFC trace with a filter of User Name = *. After your scenario has run, disable the trace and then display it. The statements beginning with the host name of your SAP NetWeaver Java server are the ones you should be interested in.

RFCs in the SAP Business Workflow system are called in the following scenarios (see the following sections): configuring and registering the system; displaying the list of work items without and with delta-pull enabled; working with substitutes; displaying the details of work items; and executing the actions of work items.

Register System

When you first register a system as a UWL provider (see "Registering Item Types" in Section 2.1), the following four RFCs are called to see if delta pull can be enabled. None of these RFCs take any import parameters; they are just called as-is and return information about the system they are running on.

▶ RPY_EXISTENCE_CHECK_CLAS
  Checks for a class to see if this is a delta-pull enabled system.

▶ UWL_DETECT_BWF_DELTA_JOB
  Checks for at least two jobs running program RSWNU-WLSEL; in other words, it is looking to see if the daily full scan and the once-a-minute delta scan jobs are there.

▶ USER_NAME_GET
  Checks for the existence of the UWL_SERVICE user.

▶ UWL_CREATE_SERVICE_USER
  Creates the UWL_SERVICE user if it did not already exist.

After the delta-pull status has been established, the next few RFCs are called to get information about the system and the workflow tasks it supports.

▶ SWN_UWL_SERVER_TYPE_DATA_GET
  Gets information about the SAP Business Workflow instance (client number, host name, etc.) and a list of transactions and task types supported by the system.

▶ SWLWP_COMP_GET_LH_URL
  Gets the left side of the launch URLs for certain tasks.

▶ SWF_VMD_METADATA_GET_ALL
  Gets the task-specific UWL customizing parameters defined in transaction SWFVISU.

Display UWL Without Delta-Pull Enabled

When a user logs in and views the worklist without delta-pull being enabled, these two RFCs get called:

▶ SWN_UWL_GET_WORKLIST
  Gets a list of work items in the user's SAP Inbox, including all information needed to display the standard UWL columns.

▶ SAP_WAPI_SUBSTITUTES_GET
  Gets a list of users for whom the current user is a substitute.

Display UWL with Delta-Pull Enabled

With delta-pull enabled for a system, the following two RFCs are called when a user views the worklist for the first time:

▶ UWL_GET_ITEMS_PROXY
  Gets all the items in a delta-pull channel since the last call.

▶ UWL_ASSIGN_USER_CHANNEL

   Assigns a user to a delta-pull channel.

Substitutions

When a user manages substitutions in the UWL, a variety of function modules, all beginning with SAP_WAPI_SUB-SITUT*, get called. There are too many to go into detail here, but their names are pretty self explanatory, and transaction SE37 will show you more details.

Substitutions are also maintained in tables in the portal database for the purposes of ad-hoc and publishing workflows. You need to be careful when adding a new SAP Business Workflow system to a productive landscape because existing substitutions from the portal will not automatically be set up in the newly added system. Similarly, in development and test scenarios, you need to make sure that all of the back end systems are active and connected when substitute maintenance is going on; otherwise, it's possible for the portal and the back end systems to get out of synch when it comes to knowing who is substituting for whom.

Display Work Item Details

When the detailed display of a work items is shown, or there are custom attributes in the UWL list view, the following RFCs are called:

▶ SAP_WAPI_GET_HEADER

   Gets the item text and metadata.

▶ SAP_WAPI_GET_OBJECTS

   Gets a list of business objects associated with the work item.

▶ UWL_SWO_INVOKE

   Gets attributes and values for a business object.

▶ SAP_WAPI_READ_CONTAINER

   Gets the attributes for the work item's container.

▶ SAP_WAPI_WORKITEM_DESCRIPTION

   Gets the long text of the work item description.

Action Handlers

This section looks at the four action handlers (see Section 2.4) that make calls to a SAP Business Workflow system when a user executes an action in UWL. The action handlers in question are the Terminating Event action handler, the Updating Container action handler, the Function Module action handler, and the default action handler.

Terminating Event Action Handler

SAP_WAPI_CREATE_EVENT is called with the object type, object ID, and event name as specified in the XML configuration.

Updating Container Action Handler

When an Updating Container action handler is called, function modules are called in the following sequence:

1. SAP_WAPI_WRITE_CONTAINER is called with the work item ID set and the SIMPLE_CONTAINER table entries set according to the <Property name="xxx" value="yyy"/> tags in the XML configuration.

2. SAP_WAPI_SET_WORKITEM_COMPLETD is called with the work item ID set; the NEW_STATUS export parameter ends up set to COMMITTED.

3. SAP_WAPI_WORKITEM_CONFIRM is called with the work item ID set.

Function Module Action Handler

The function module specified in the XML configuration file is called, with the parameters specified in the configuration.

Default Action Handler

If no other action handler is specified, the default action for SAP Business Workflow work items is to launch transaction SWK1 with a Web GUI. This transaction figures out what would have happened if the user clicked on the work item in the SAP Inbox and fires off the appropriate SAP transaction to handle that item, so it is a safe default for the majority of cases.

5.4 Technical Considerations

In this section, you will see that although UWL is a very powerful tool, there are still some areas where you need to think before using it as the default front end for a SAP Business Workflow system. Some of these areas are specific to UWL, and some are related to your choice of SAP GUI to launch for items that are handled using standard SAP transactions.

SAP Business Workflow

The main difference from using the SAP Inbox to launch items is *chained execution*. This is where completion of one work item naturally leads to the same agent processing another. Using SAP Inbox, the user is taken transparently to the next work item processing screen, giving the nice illusion of a single piece of work where there are multiple work items. UWL does not have this technology, and the user needs to go back to the work list and refresh it after completing each individual work item.

Luckily, one area where work item chaining is common has been addressed by SAP: Users can enter a comment for generic decision items using a UWL-specific user interface (this would normally have been done with a chained item asking for a comment after the decision). See "User Decision Handler" in Section 3.2 for details.

Most of the other technical considerations are related to the use of SAP GUI for HTML for launching work items from UWL. These considerations are covered in the next sections.

> **Tip**
>
> Up-to-date information on how UWL operates with SAP Business Workflow is contained in SAP Note 794439 ("Universal Worklist Support for SAP Business Workflow".)

SAP GUI for HTML (WebGUI)

You can find the main limitations of the SAP GUI for HTML described in SAP Note 314568, "SAP GUI for HTML functionality/Limitations/Sp. Behavior" and SAP Note 300645, "Up/Download Functions in ITS Context". The aspects that have an impact on UWL are as follows:

No New Sessions or Windows

A Web GUI session cannot launch any new GUI windows or sessions, so, for example, a user who tries to launch a transaction in a new window using /0 will get a message that no new sessions are allowed. Sometimes there is a button in a transaction that will try and launch a new session; if that transaction is launched for processing a work item, then you need to either use a Windows GUI for that item's task type or train your users to avoid pressing the button.

File Upload/Download Requires Java VM

If the transaction launched to handle a work item involves the ability to upload or download files (e.g., scanned invoices), the Web GUI uses a Java applet in the browser to control the file upload/download behavior. This applet requires a Sun Java VM (virtual machine) to be installed on the client PC (see SAP Note 980772). The Microsoft VM that comes installed with Internet Explorer will not do the job. This means that you may have to arrange for a Sun Java VM to be installed on all of your users' machines.

If the downloaded file requires an application to view it (e.g., a PDF file, TIFF image, or Word document), then users will be prompted to browse the file system of their PC for the appropriate executable file to handle that document type. This can be tricky, as many users do not necessarily know the location of the executable files. The users' choice is stored in the file execookie.txt so that they do not have to search for an executable each time, but this can come with its own problems if the software is upgraded because a new version of the executable could well be in a new folder.

One solution to this is to use an automatic software deployment tool for all software upgrades to your users so that whenever a new version of a package is deployed, you can deploy an updated execookie.txt file to them at the same time.

SAP GUI for Java (JavaGUI)

Although a Java VM is required on the client PC to run the Java GUI, the same can be said for the Web GUI if any file upload/download activity is being carried out. Other than that, the Java GUI is almost as good as the Windows GUI, with fewer limitations than the Web GUI. After the Java GUI has been downloaded through the browser, it is more bandwidth-efficient than the Web GUI, and may well be a good choice for UWL work item processing.

On the down side, the Java GUI is not widely used, it can be a bit of an unknown (so getting support from SAP Developer Network forums and so on may be harder), it is a little more tricky to deploy than the HTML or Windows GUIs, and development tends to lag behind Web/Win GUI releases. The Java GUI is a much better solution than it used to be, however, and is actually a realistic GUI choice for Mac OS X or UNIX users who are not able to run a Windows GUI.

> **Tip**
>
> See SAP Note 454939 "SAP GUI for Java Limitations" for the latest information on the Java GUI.

SAP GUI for Windows

The main disadvantage of using the SAP GUI for Windows (Win GUI) is that it needs to be installed locally on each user's PC and kept up to date. When you are deploying a portal-based solution, one of the main selling points is that it is almost entirely a browser-based solution, so when you have to then go and install dedicated client software on each PC, it takes away most of the main advantage of using such a solution.

Specifically for UWL, there is an issue with the system definition in the Portal System Landscape you may need to be careful of when using Win GUI transactions. The SAP Connector properties for a UWL system are used for the portal server to talk to the SAP Business Workflow server. The same set of properties is used to generate the SAP shortcut for launching a GUI session from the user's PC. The problem can arise where the connection a SAP Business Workflow server in the data center (for the server-to-server connection) may not be the same as for the client-to-server connection, which often goes via a

SAProuter. In these cases, you need to configure the portal to SAP Business Workflow server connection also to use a SAProuter, and the SAProuter must allow that particular routing.

Of course, if the connections are in place, and the SAP GUI software is installed on your users' PCs, then the Windows GUI will give the best performance and the least amount of trouble when processing work items from UWL.

5.5   Summary

In this chapter, you've seen what really makes UWL tick. First, you saw the SAP-provided tools for troubleshooting the UWL, namely the Support Information option on the UWL iView and the SAP NetWeaver Java log files. Next, you learned how to get the best performance out of UWL: delta-pull is highly recommended, as is specifying roles for systems if you have more than one back end system connected. After that, we got a bit unofficial as you saw the results of a number of RFC-tracing exercises to see exactly which function modules get called by UWL as it goes about its business. Finally you saw that UWL is not quite a 100 % replacement for the SAP Inbox and learned what you need to think about when deploying UWL and the various types of SAP GUI to make your implementation successful.

6 Next-Generation Workflow

Until this point, this book has described UWL as a way of enabling users to engage in business processes and workflows using the SAP NetWeaver Portal. In this chapter, we'll look at some new technologies and techniques from SAP that make these processes and workflows usable from outside of the normal SAP ecosystem.

All of the methods in this chapter are made possible through SAP's commitment to an enterprise service-oriented architecture (enterprise SOA). Enterprise SOA is a business-driven software architecture that increases adaptability, flexibility, openness, and cost-efficiency. With enterprise SOA, organizations can compose applications and enable business processes rapidly using enterprise services, improve their reuse of software, and become more agile in responding to change.

The chapter starts with a brief overview of the concepts behind enterprise services (see Section 6.1) and then dives straight into the detail with a workshop showing you how to process SAP Business Workflow items on a BlackBerry handheld device (see Section 6.2). Following the workshop, there are a couple of sections where you will get a high-level overview of how an enterprise services approach enables the technologies of SAP NetWeaver Voice (see Section 6.3) and Duet (see Section 6.4), which allow SAP to interact with the telephone system and Microsoft Outlook, respectively.

6.1 Business Processes and Enterprise Services

Enterprise SOA has its technical roots in the concepts behind service-oriented architectures (SOA). SOA involves the capability of different systems to produce and consume services using a standards-based infrastructure such as the Web Services stack of UDDI, WSDL, and

SOAP; these acronyms are explained next, following which you will learn about some of the emerging standards for enterprise services dealing with business processes and workflow modeling.

Standards for Web Services: SOAP, WSDL, and UDDI
The acronyms surrounding Web Services can be confusing at first, so here's a simple description of what they mean:

▶ SOAP
Originally standing for Simple Object Access Protocol, now Service-Oriented Architecture Protocol (see *http://www.w3.org/TR/ws-arch/#SOAP*), SOAP is a method for calling Web Services using XML messages to describe the service name, calling parameters, and returned results. These messages are normally passed around using the Web standard protocols HTTP/HTTPS but can also be sent in emails and other message delivery systems.

▶ WSDL
The Web Services Description Language is used to describe SOAP services and is analogous to the ABAP Data Dictionary. A WSDL document can describe the number and type of all calling and return parameters for a service and can also be used to validate the correctness of an incoming SOAP request.

▶ UDDI
Universal Description, Discovery, and Integration is used to locate Web Services. If there is a particular Web Service you want to call, you can query a UDDI server to find out where that service is being provided.

The Web Services stack works as follows: First, you query your local UDDI directory to find somewhere providing the service you are interested in. You then request the WSDL from that service provider to discover the precise syntax of the service. Finally, you construct a SOAP call using that syntax to actually use the service.

Business Process Modeling Standards: BPML, BPEL, and BPEL4People

To explain BPEL4People, it's best to start by talking about BPEL and BPML. BPEL (Business Process Execution Language) and BPML (Business Process Modeling Language) are both standards for modeling business processes and workflows.

▶ BPML is an older standard, now obsolete because the standard's developer, the BPMI (Business Process Modeling Institute), dropped support for it in favor of BPEL. SAP Business Workflow process models can be exported from SAP GUI as BPML files.

▶ BPEL is an executable language that runs on compatible workflow engines and allows processes to access multiple systems using Web Services. One such engine is the Process Integration (PI) component of SAP NetWeaver.

BPEL4People, from IBM and SAP, extends the BPEL standard to allow for the notion of human tasks. Although SAP NetWeaver PI is very good at orchestrating processes among several systems, it is only really comfortable with machines as process participants. BPEL4People's notion of human tasks, and the related notions of roles and groups of people and a people-centric task list, maps nicely onto a combination of UWL, GPs consuming Web Services, and the PI engine. At the time of writing, the BPEL4People specification had only just been standardized and had not yet been formally implemented by SAP, but it may well be part of the further development of SAP NetWeaver.

One way in which BPEL4People is relevant to UWL is that after a third-party UWL connector (see Chapter 4) is developed to read tasks from a BPEL4People engine, then the standards-based nature of BPEL4People means that any business process management system supporting the standard will automatically be able to present its tasks in UWL.

6.2   Workshop: Workflow on a BlackBerry

The RIM BlackBerry series of handheld devices are becoming increasingly popular in business. Most people use them simply as mobile email devices, but they also have web browsers built in and can also run standalone Java applications. You wouldn't want to try and run a SAP GUI or a portal on one of these devices, but when a decision needs to be made, you can get the relevant information out to the user and feed their decision back into the SAP Business Workflow system.

We're going to carry on with the notification of absence workflow shown in earlier chapters. We'll actually use the Web Dynpro application from Chapter 3 to display the details of the absence and get the manager's decision.

One of the great features of Web Dynpro Java is that a BlackBerry device is automatically detected, and content is rendered appropriately in WML instead of in HTML. WML (Wireless Markup Language), is a simplified page markup language for mobile devices; think of it as a kind of HTML for small screens. The other key element that makes this scenario work is the use of SAP's single sign-on module for BlackBerry handhelds, which comes as part of SAP CRM.

Here's how the scenario works (shown diagrammatically in Figure 6.1):

1. After a user has submitted a notification of absence, the SAP Business Workflow system sends an email to the approver.

2. The approver receives this email on the BlackBerry device.

3. The approver clicks on a link in the email.

4. This link launches the BlackBerry browser, which then accesses the Web Dynpro application on the portal server.

5. The user is automatically logged on to the portal server by SAP's BlackBerry login module.

6. The Web Dynpro application gets the details of the absence request from the SAP Business Workflow system and shows them to the approver, along with **Approve** and **Reject** links.

7. The approver selects one of the links.

8. The Web Dynpro application responds to the selection and notifies the SAP Business Workflow system of the approver's decision.

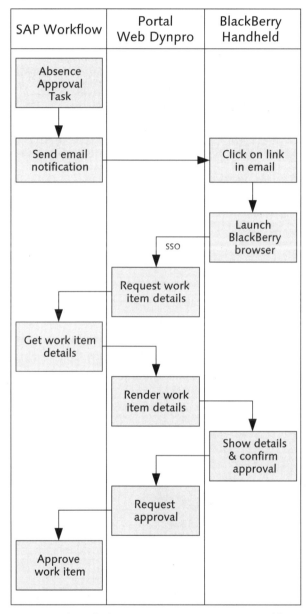

Figure 6.1   Flow of Information Between SAP Business Workflow, Portal Web Dynpro, and BlackBerry Handheld Device

In the rest of the section, we'll go through the steps necessary to get the preceding scenario working. As well as a SAP NetWeaver Developer Studio, you will find it useful to have instances of the BlackBerry Java Development Environment (JDE) (which contains a BlackBerry device simulator), the BlackBerry Email Service Simulator (ESS),

and the BlackBerry Mobile Data Service (MDS) Simulator. With these, you will be able to test the application without actually requiring a BlackBerry handheld device (if you have a BlackBerry already, you can use it for testing by connecting it to your development PC via a USB cable and the BlackBerry Desktop Connect software that comes with the device). The simulators are all freely downloadable from Research in Motion[1]; version 4.1.2 of each package is used in these examples.

Setting Up a BlackBerry Test Environment
Before you can develop anything for the BlackBerry, it makes sense to get a working BlackBerry simulator up and running, which you can do as follows:

1. Download and install the BlackBerry JDE.
2. Download and install the BlackBerry Email and MDS Services Simulators.
3. Find the ESS configuration file `rimpublic.property` in the folder *C:\Program Files\Research In Motion\BlackBerry Email and MDS Services Simulators 4.1.2\ESS\ config*.
4. Edit the four properties in Table 6.1 in the ESS `rimpublic.property` file. These settings will allow the BlackBerry simulator to send and receive emails.

Property Name	Description
`Email.pop3Server`	Address of the incoming email POP3 server
`Email.smtpServer`	Address of the outgoing SMTP server
`Email.personal`	Your name
`Email.address`	Your email address

Table 6.1   Settings for the ESS rimpublic.property file

5. Find the Mobile Data Service (MDS) Simulator configuration file `rimpublic.property` in the folder *C:\Program Files\Research In Motion\BlackBerry Email and MDS Services Simulators 4.1.2\MDS\config*.
6. Edit the properties shown in Table 6.2 in the MDS `rimpublic.property` file. These settings will enable

---

1 You can download the BlackBerry Java Development Environment from *http://na.blackberry.com/eng/developers/downloads*, by selecting the menu **BlackBerry Java Development Environment**. The BlackBerry Email and MDS Services Simulator Package is available from the same address, by selecting the menu **BlackBerry Simulators**.

single sign-on by adding your email address to HTTP request headers.

Table 6.2 Settings for the MDS rimpublic.property file

Property Name	Description
Simulator. 2100000a	The default value is MDS, simulator@pushme.com; change the email address to your email address.
application.handler.http.header	Set the value to email.

7. Run the ESS, enter the user name and password to access your POP3 server (see the upcoming box "Using a Local Mail Server for Testing" if you don't have a POP3/SMTP server), set a poll interval of 60 seconds (see Figure 6.2), and click the **Launch** button.

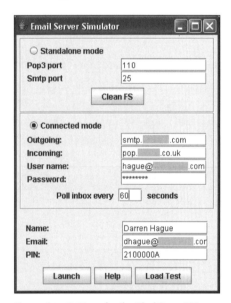

Figure 6.2   Settings for the BlackBerry ESS

Using a Local Mail Server for Testing

For the purposes of development and testing, you may find it convenient to install your own SMTP/POP3 server such as the Mercury Mail Transport System freely available from *http://www.pmail.com*. Using your own server in this way means that your test emails stay within a "walled garden," and you can set up email accounts for your test users that can be accessed easily from both the BlackBerry handheld device simulator and your desktop email client.

8. Start the BlackBerry MDS simulator; this will appear as a Windows console application with a stream of logging messages (see Figure 6.3).

Figure 6.3   Running the BlackBerry MDS Simulator

9. Start the BlackBerry device simulator. By doing so, run the setup wizard the first time, but tell it to skip email setup when asked.

10. Now check that email is working: Send an email to your POP3 account and wait for a minute. You should see a notification appear and the red LED at the top-right on the BlackBerry simulator will start flashing (see Figure 6.4). You should be able to scroll down, select the **Messages** icon ( ), and view the email you just sent to this account. A star on the Messages icon should illustrate this. If you have any difficulties at this stage, it may help to download and run the BlackBerry Desktop Connect software from RIM.

Figure 6.4   BlackBerry Device Simulator

11. Check that you can access the Internet: Scroll down and click the **Applications** icon (▦), and then select the **Browser** icon (🌐). Click the **Menu** button on the device keyboard (▦), select the menu item **Go To...**, and enter "http://www.google.com." After a few seconds, you should see the Google home page (assuming your PC is online, of course).

If all of that worked correctly, you now have everything you need to test BlackBerry applications with email and web connectivity.

Check Access to the Web Dynpro Application from a BlackBerry

Now that you have the test environment set up, you can use it to access the Web Dynpro application from Section 3.3.1. The clever thing here is that no changes to the Web Dynpro application are needed to make it work on a BlackBerry.

1. Create an Absence Approval work item (see Chapter 3 for details), and note the work item ID from the approver's Inbox.

2. Launch the BlackBerry browser, and go to the application with the work item ID passed as a parameter, for example, *http://<server name>:50000/webdynpro/ dispatcher/local/AbsenceApproval/AbsenceApproval? wi_id=13007*.

Tip

If you copy the link and paste it into the BlackBerry simulator, you may notice that the capital "A" letters in the link do not get pasted in, so you will have to edit the URL and enter these manually.

3. You will see a logon screen, where you should enter the approver's user name and password (see Figure 6.5).

4. After you have entered a user name and password, you should see the Web Dynpro application (see Figure 6.6) displaying the details of the absence, along with links (from the Web Dynpro buttons) for approving or rejecting the absence.

5. If you select the **Reject** link, you should get a confirmation screen like the one in Figure 6.7.

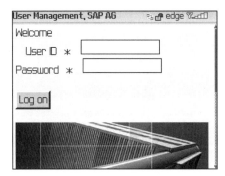

Figure 6.5   Web Dynpro Login Screen Shown on a BlackBerry

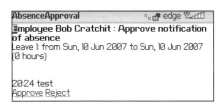

Figure 6.6   Web Dynpro Application Shown on a BlackBerry

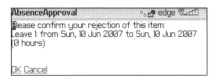

Figure 6.7   Confirmation Check Screen

6. Finally, clicking **OK** confirms the decision and leads to the screen shown in Figure 6.8.

Figure 6.8   Final Screen Showing Success Message

Configure Workflow Step to Send Email

For the SAP Business Workflow system to send emails to an email client such as a BlackBerry handheld device, you need to carry out the following steps:

1. Run transaction SCOT, and double-click on the **SMTP** node. In the resulting pop-up, set the mail host address to the name of your SMTP server.

2. Still in transaction SCOT, select **View • Jobs** (or use the F8 key), and create a new job "Send mail," selecting the variant **SAP&CONNECTINT** (sending Internet requests). Schedule this job to run every 5 minutes.

3. If you need more details on fine-tuning this configuration, see the SAP Help Portal entry **SAPconnect (BC-SRV-COM) • Administration • Settings for Sending Using the SMTP Plug-In**.

Now that the system is set up to send emails, let's move on to configure the notification of absence workflow for email notification. Here we're going through the procedure that is documented in more detail in the SAP Help Portal entry **Embedded Processes (SAP Business Workflow) • Integration • Enabling Communication • Extended Notifications for SAP Business Workflow • Typical Use Cases and Examples • Example: Notifications for Leave Requests.**

1. Start by running transaction SWNADMIN, and choose the scenario **WORKFLOW**.
2. Create a category ZLEAVEREQUEST.
3. Select the new category from the list, and then click on the **Selection** menu. Create a selection, also called ZLEAVEREQUEST, and assign it to the category of the same name.
4. After you've created the selection, go to the **Tasks** tab, and assign the tasks for which you want an email to be sent; in this case, TS30000016 for the email to the approver, TS30000102 for the notification of the approver's decision, and TS00008267 for the decision task for the initiator to decide what to do about a rejection. You can see the outcome of this in Figure 6.9.

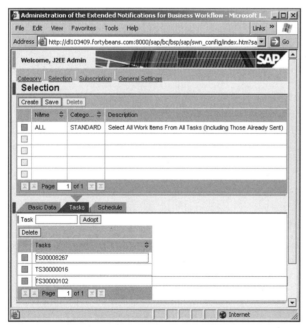

Figure 6.9   Creating a Selection of Tasks for Email Notification

5. Go to the **Schedule** tab, and set a schedule of every 5 minutes every day for new/changed items, and 9am each day for all items, and then save the Selection.
6. Create a subscription to the category for which the selection has been defined. Select the **Subscription** menu and create a subscription ZLEAVEREQUEST to the category of the same name.
7. Go to the **Message** tab, and select a **Delivery Type** of **Text-Only Message** and a **Message Granularity** of **One Message per Work Item**. Go to the **Schedule** tab, set up a schedule of every 5 minutes, and then go to the **Recipient** tab and make sure the subscription is valid for all users. Finally, save the subscription.
8. Select the **General Settings** menu, and make sure that the host name of the ITS and Web Dynpro servers are filled in.
9. Use transaction SE38 to schedule a job to run report SWN_SELSEN every 5 minutes (you may have to create a variant for the default attribute **No time check during send**).

> **Important Note**
>
> The value of 5 minutes used several times in the previous paragraph is for development purposes only to make sure you get quick feedback. In a test or production system, these values are more likely to be in the 15 to 30 minute range.

Customize the Workflow Email to Contain a Link to the Web Dynpro Application

All you need to do now is customize the SAP Business Workflow task description (which gets sent out in the email) so that it contains a link to run the Web Dynpro application.

1. Run transaction SWDD to edit workflow WS30000015, and select the step **Approve notification of absence** (see Figure 6.10).
2. Double-click on the task ID (TS30000016) to edit the task, and on the resulting screen, select the **Description** tab.
3. Click the **Change text** icon (🖉) to edit the text.
4. Remove the text "If you reject the request, create an attachment explaining your reason for the rejection."

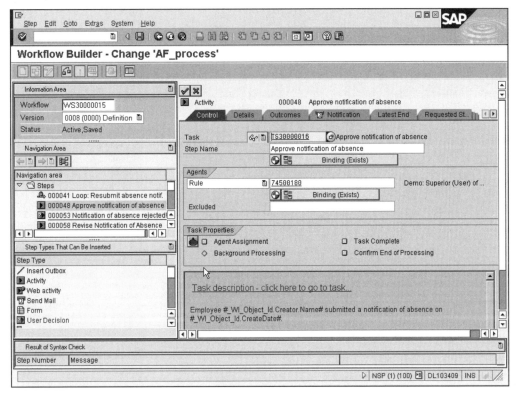

Figure 6.10   Select the Approval Step in the Workflow

and replace it with "Make a decision about the request by selecting the following link:"

5. Add a link to the Web Dynpro application, including the wi_id parameter but not including the value, for example:

   http://<server name>:50000/webdynpro/dispatcher/local/AbsenceApproval/AbsenceApproval?wi_id=

6. Position the cursor after the link, and select **Insert • Expression**. In the resulting dialog box, select **Container • Step • Work Item ID**. The text should now look like Figure 6.11.

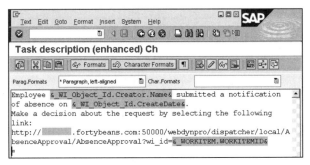

Figure 6.11   Changing the Work Item Description for Task TS30000016

7. Go back to the workflow definition, and then save and activate ⬛ the workflow.

Test the Workflow Email to the BlackBerry

Now that you have configured SAP Business Workflow to send emails and have customized the task description, it's time to test that this works correctly.

> **Note**
>
> The test assumes that your BlackBerry device or simulator is set up with the same email address as the approver in the workflow.

1. Log in to the SAP Business Workflow system (as Bob Cratchit in this example), and run transaction SWXF to create a notification of absence (see Figure 6.12).

2. Wait for 10 minutes or so for the SAP Business Workflow email batch jobs (defined previously) to run, and then check the BlackBerry device or simulator. If using the simulator, first make sure that the ESS and MDS

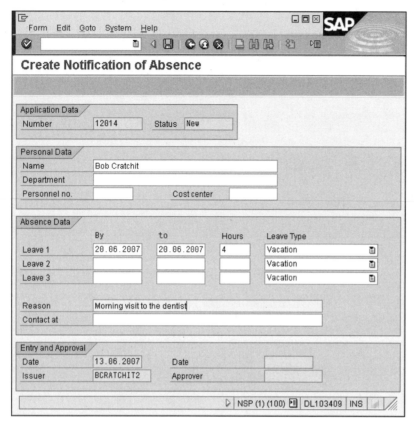

Figure 6.12 Creating a Notification of Absence with SWXF

services are running. You should see the email notification arrive, as shown in Figure 6.13.

Figure 6.13 Incoming Email from SAP Business Workflow

3. Open the email, and you should see a brief description of the work item and an underlined link (see Figure 6.14).

Employee Bob Cratchit : Approve notification
of absence

Employee Bob Cratchit submitted a notification
of absence on 10.06.2007.
Make a decision about the request by selecting
the following link:
http://uk01138.fortybeans.com:50000/
webdynpro/dispatcher/local/AbsenceApproval/
AbsenceApproval?wi_id=000000014036

Figure 6.14 Body of Email Received on the BlackBerry

4. If you select the link, it should launch the BlackBerry browser and take you to the login screen shown earlier (refer to Figure 6.5), and you should be able to log in and test the application in the same way as before.

Now that you have successfully shown the application working from an email on the BlackBerry, the last thing to do is get single sign-on working so that there is no need for users to log in each time they want to approve an item.

Configure Single Sign-on from BlackBerry to SAP

SAP provides a login module to allow single sign-on from a BlackBerry handheld device as part of SAP CRM Mobile Sales.

1. You can get hold of this module (if you have a SAP Service Marketplace login) by going to *http://service.sap.com/swdc* and searching for "MSON."

2. You should find **MSON 1.0** in the search results. Click this link, and then drill down to the **#OS independent**

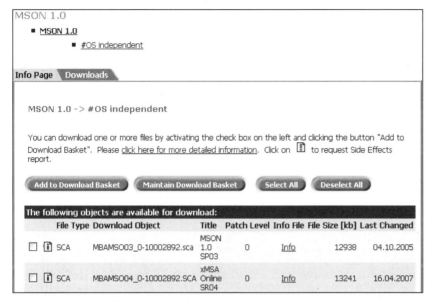

Figure 6.15   Locating the SAP CRM Mobile Sales Module

level of navigation. Figure 6.15 shows how this navigation appeared at the time of writing.

3. Download the latest version of the module, then open the SCA file using a ZIP extraction program such as WinZip, and extract the file `mba~com.sap.mbs.ca.rimloginlibrary.sda`. This is SAP's BlackBerry login module, which you should deploy to the server where the Web Dynpro application is running.

Next, configure the Login Module stack as follows:

1. Launch Visual Administrator, and go to **Server 0 • Services • Security Provider**.

2. Select the **Properties** tab, and add the following value to the key **LoginModuleClassLoaders**:
   `library:mba~com.sap.mbs.ca.rimloginlibrary`

3. Go to the **Runtime** tab, select the **User Management** tab beneath it, and then click the **Switch to edit mode** icon (🖉) to go to edit mode.

4. Click the **Manage Security Stores** button (see Figure 6.16).

5. With the UME User Store selected, click the **Add Login Module** button, and then click **OK** to the dialog box requesting an editor.

6. In the **Add Login Module** dialog box, enter a class name of `com.sap.mbs.ca.RIMAuthentication.RIMLoginModule` and a display name of `RIMLoginModule`, and then click **OK**.

7. Select the **Policy Configurations** tab, and from the list of components, select **ticket**.

8. Click the **Add New** button, and select `RIMLoginModule` from the list of available login modules. It will then appear at the bottom of the list of login modules; select it, and click **Modify**.

9. Change the Position to **2**, and set the Flag to **OPTIONAL**.

10. Similarly, click the **Add New** button once again, select `CreateTicketLoginModule`, and modify it to have a Position of **3**, a Flag of **SUFFICIENT**, and an option name of `ume.configuration.active` with a value of **true**. This should lead to a login module stack that looks something like Figure 6.17.

11. Restart the J2EE Server node to activate this configuration.

The `RIMLoginModule` works by looking for the BlackBerry user's email address in the HTTP request header variable `Rim-device-email`. The module then uses the SAP UME to find the first user with this email address, and it puts the corresponding user ID into the JAAS (Java Authentication and Authorization Service) login context.

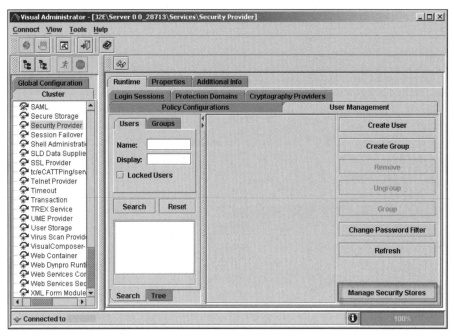

Figure 6.16 The Manage Security Stores Button

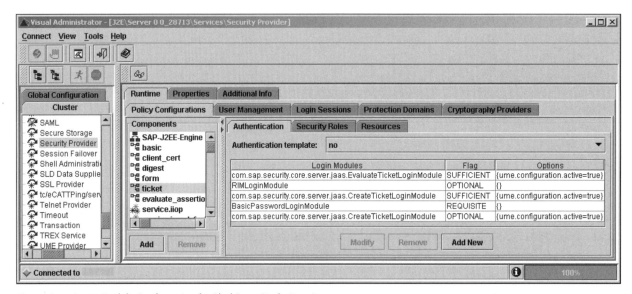

Figure 6.17 Login Module Configuration for BlackBerry Single Sign-On

CreateTicketLoginModule looks in the login context. If it finds no user ID, then it returns fail, and no user is logged in (unless they pass the BasicPasswordLoginModule). If it does find a user ID in the login context, then it creates a SAP login ticket for that user and returns success. Because this module has the **SUFFICIENT** flag set, the logon stack is terminated at this point, and the user is logged in.

To test single sign-on using the BlackBerry simulator, make sure that in the rimpublic.property file for the BlackBerry MDS simulator you have set the property Simulator.2100000a to the email address of a work item approver (as described in "Setting Up a BlackBerry Test Environment" in Section 6.2). You should now be able to access the Web Dynpro application using the BlackBerry browser as shown in the previous section, but this time you should be automatically logged in.

You can check the progress of the BlackBerry login module by telling the J2EE Log Configurator to monitor the category /Libraries/RIMLoginModule or the location com.sap.mbs.ca.RIMAuthentication.

As a result of all the steps in this workshop, BlackBerry users will be notified of work items needing their attention, and they will be able to act on those items with just a few clicks of the BlackBerry action button.

6.3   SAP NetWeaver Voice

SAP NetWeaver Voice is a part of the SAP NetWeaver Composition Environment (SAP NetWeaver CE), a part of SAP NetWeaver 7.1 and later, and allows you to create SAP applications that work with the telephone system using SOA techniques. Rather than going into workshop-level detail on SAP NetWeaver Voice, in this section we're just going to have a high-level look at what SAP NetWeaver Voice is, how it works, and how you can go about integrating it with a SAP Business Workflow system or GPs to allow your users to work with business processes by telephone.

Most telephone applications run on dedicated servers that know how to talk to PSTN (Public Switched Telephone Network) and VoIP (Voice over Internet Protocol) telephone networks. These servers support a language called VoiceXML, which is the W3C standard XML format for specifying interactive voice dialogues between a human and a computer. As well as being capable of recognizing and synthesizing speech, VoiceXML can also deal with DTMF tone responses (the "touch-tones" you get when you press the keys on your telephone). SAP NetWeaver Voice allows you to deploy applications to VoiceXML-compliant telephony servers and allows those applications to talk back to SAP NetWeaver (see Figure 6.18).

All of this is made quite straightforward for the application developer. SAP provides a Voice Kit for SAP NetWeaver Visual Composer that allows you to develop SAP NetWeaver applications with Voice-interactive elements. The phone is treated like a basic web browser with the ability to make requests, get responses, and post form data (by speaking or using touch-tones). To the application server, this is done using VoiceXML documents; the voice gateway then translates between VoiceXML and actual voice prompts and responses.

How to Get Started with SAP NetWeaver Voice

You will need an instance of the SAP NetWeaver Composition Environment server and the SAP NetWeaver CE version of the SAP NetWeaver Developer Studio. For development purposes, you can download a trial version of these from the SAP Developer Network by going to *https://www.sdn.sap.com/irj/sdn/nw-ce* and following the link to **SAP NetWeaver Composition Environment Downloads**.

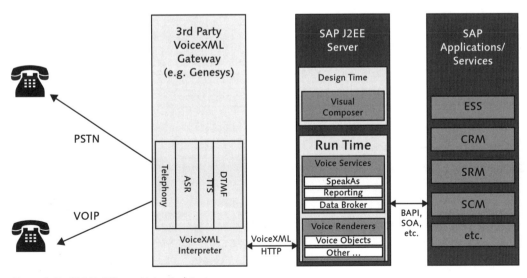

Figure 6.18   SAP NetWeaver Voice Architecture

For a VoiceXML-compatible gateway to use with SAP NetWeaver Voice, you can use Voxeo's Prophecy software, which is available from *http://www.voxeo.com/prophecy* and allows you to handle up to two concurrent calls for free. This software comes with a SIP "softphone," which allows you to simulate a telephone on your PC using its microphone and headphone jacks, and will also work with VoIP calls over the Internet. If you want to set up a really impressive demo to an actual physical telephone, you can try hooking up a VoIP-PSTN gateway; *http://www.voipuser.org* has one that you can use free for experimental purposes that will allow you to dial out to phones in several countries for no charge (or a small Pay-Pal donation) and will also give you a UK-based telephone number that you can connect back into a SIP (Session Initiation Protocol) client (SIP is a standard in Internet telephony).

You need to configure SAP NetWeaver CE to enable SAP NetWeaver Voice and to integrate it with Voxeo Prophecy. The instructions for doing this are in the SAP Help Portal at **SAP NetWeaver Composition Environment Library • Administrator's Guide • Configuration for CE Additional Components • Configuring Voice-Enabled Applications**. The VoiceXML gateway driver to use is number 89, "Voxeo Prophecy Voice Platform 7.0."

Workflow Integration

SAP NetWeaver Voice applications produced by Visual Composer are like other web applications in that they are started by a request from an end user, in this case, by an incoming phone call to the VoiceXML gateway. However, for a workflow situation, you want the system to place a call to a user when the user is required to take an action.

A good example of this is when the "Latest start" deadline is reached in an SAP Business Workflow decision step, we want to call the user to get an immediate decision. This can deliver significant business benefits by making sure that a purchase order is approved before it is too late for a supplier to ship goods on time for a business-critical activity. Where a decision maker might not act on a notification email for a number of hours, the person is much more likely to pick up on an incoming phone call, listen to a description of the purchase order, and answer "yes" when asked to approve it.

The solution is to make use of the VoiceXML gateway's capability to place outgoing calls in response to an HTTP request. There is a guide to doing this with Voxeo Prophecy at *http://www.prophecy2006.com/node/23*. Basically, you write a short script in another language supported by voice gateways CCXML (Call Control eXtensible Markup Language), which is used to control calls and initiate VoiceXML applications. This CCXML script can be fired by making an HTTP request, so you just need to configure a workflow step in the "Missed Deadline" branch of your workflow to initiate this request and pass in the work item ID and the user's phone number as parameters. The CCXML script that gets called will then dial the user and pass control to the SAP NetWeaver Voice application, which can use the work item ID to find out the necessary task data using the SAP_WAPI function modules.

Authentication

As with any application accessing a core ERP system, you will probably want to make sure that users are properly authenticated. You can't use the normal Java authentication methods with SAP NetWeaver Voice; instead, you should add a voice authentication block to the start of each application you develop. This block should ask the user for the user ID and a numeric PIN and can then call an RFC of your choice to validate this information before allowing the application to proceed.

SAP Documentation

You can find detailed documentation on developing voice applications with SAP NetWeaver Visual Composer at the SAP Help Portal in the section **SAP NetWeaver Composition Environment Library • Developer's Guide • Developing and Composing Applications • Developing Voice-Enabled Applications.** The SAP Developer Network has a good white paper available (see Table B.5 in Appendix B for link details).

6.4   Duet: Business Processes in Microsoft Outlook

Duet is the name of the SAP and Microsoft product for integrating SAP systems with Microsoft Office. Based on a SOA, Duet is intended to become an open platform for allowing access to back end business systems and information sources from Microsoft-based desktop clients, but in its current stage of evolution, it delivers a number of preintegrated scenarios from SAP.

Of interest to us here is how Microsoft Outlook could potentially be used as an alternative UWL. From an end-user point of view, it can sometimes be hard to explain why the "business inbox" is split into two. The user must go to UWL to see items from back end systems, but all of the other items (including those from customers and coworkers) appear in the Outlook inbox. Duet offers a way out of this by ultimately being able to provide access to all inbox items from the same place: Microsoft Outlook.

Although it is currently possible to send notifications of work items to someone's email inbox and to process them from there via links to web applications or by replying to notifications, there are some weaknesses with these approaches. For example, with SAP SRM's offline approval option, an email notification for a shopping cart approval is sent containing two links: one for approve and one for reject. These links generate reply emails that are then processed by SAP SRM to carry out the approval. The dangers with this approach are the following:

▸ There is nothing to stop two replies being sent, an approval *and* a rejection.

▸ There is no secure method of authentication; the original email may be forwarded to someone else who then carries out the approval (although they would need to have the same sender address), and there is no way of auditing this or even knowing if the approver is authorized or not (a PA may manage a director's emails, and this PA could then both raise and approve a requisition).

If you are not using Duet, but you do want a form of email-based approval, the only safe way is for the email notification to include a link to UWL, which then guarantees correct security and functionality.

A Duet-integrated workflow scenario would connect to the back end SAP system as soon as a user opens the item in the inbox. In a future incarnation where Outlook replaces UWL[2], it's possible that the item may only be in the inbox as a result of talking to the SAP system in the first place, instead of relying on an email being sent. In

this situation, all information is current all of the time; the approver will be looking at the current status of the requisition (which may have been changed by the requisitioner since the original submission), and any approval will happen immediately in the SAP system in a properly authenticated and auditable manner, without the need to click a link, launch a browser, and wait for an application to load.

Duet Workflow Scenarios
Next we're going to look at some of the business process-related scenarios that are implemented in Duet release 1.5 (the current release at the time of writing). There will surely be more scenarios delivered in future releases. SOA means that the core ERP system need hardly be touched to do so.

Travel Management and Leave Management
In these two scenarios, an employee can construct a travel plan or leave request in the SAP system from the Duet client, having started by blocking out the time as an appointment in the Outlook calendar. After the employee submits the travel plan or leave request for approval, the manager gets an email notification.

On opening the email, the Duet Action Pane displays the current request status alongside a BI report showing the available travel budget (for the travel plan) and gives access to related reports, a copy of the local travel or leave policy, and business process-related help from a knowledge base. Buttons in the toolbar of the email window allow the manager to approve or reject the request there and then.

Purchasing Management
In this scenario, a user raises a shopping cart in SAP SRM. An email notification is sent to the user's manager, who opens it in Outlook. At this point, the Duet Action Pane opens and shows a summary of the shopping cart, the remaining budget for the relevant cost center, the list of approvers in the approval chain, and a list of related links to the purchasing policy and various SRM-related reports. The manager can enter a note in a text box in the Duet

---

2 There is no official SAP statement intending to allow Outlook to be used instead of UWL in this way, but it's an interesting idea and the kind of thing that SOA makes possible.

pane before clicking on an **Approve** or **Reject** button in the email's toolbar to notify the SAP SRM system of the approval immediately.

Recruitment Management
This scenario integrates with SAP's eRecruitment solution to generate an Outlook task for an interviewer to fill in a questionnaire after interviewing a candidate. The questionnaire itself is presented as a tab in the task window, and the Duet Action Pane gives access to various sets of related information such as the candidate's application form and CV (résumé), the recruiting process overview, and applicable policies and guidelines.

This is the equivalent of a more transactional type of work item being completed in Outlook instead of the simpler approve/reject decision items described so far.

Duet Architecture and Infrastructure Requirements

A Duet implementation is designed to be deployed into a system landscape that already consists of a SAP ERP system, a Microsoft network using Active Directory coupled with an Exchange Server for email and groupware, and a desktop environment based on Microsoft Office 2003 and Microsoft .NET 2.0. With these elements already in place, all that is required to implement Duet is to arrange for the installation of a Duet client add-on for the desktop environment, and the deployment of a Duet server environment, which can be a single box running SAP NetWeaver on Windows 2003 server onto which is deployed a Duet Server component and a Duet SAP Add-On component (these can be installed on separate boxes for scalability if required, see Figure 6.19). This Duet server is then configured to talk to the Microsoft Active Directory and Exchange environments as well as the SAP ERP instance.

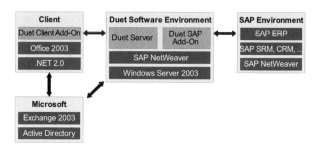

Figure 6.19   Duet Architecture

6.5   Summary

In this chapter, you've learned how SAP's enterprise SOA, a business process-level approach to SOA, has enabled the deployment of cross-system business processes in a number of interesting new ways. Enterprise SOA makes it much easier to integrate new technologies as they appear (BlackBerry, Voice, and Microsoft Office), and SAP NetWeaver acts as a platform to develop new business process technologies such as Guided Procedures (GP), which in itself uses (enterprise) SOA to allow the simple creation of processes that cross system boundaries. Integrating these new technologies is so easy that in the case of GPs and SAP NetWeaver Voice, new processes can be developed and deployed without even writing any code.

This chapter has shown that while UWL is a way of bringing a user's tasks from multiple systems into one place, the SAP NetWeaver Portal, enterprise SOA takes this a step further and enables tasks and work items to be delivered to a place of the users' choosing. This means that when new processes and systems are deployed, their adoption rate is likely to be much higher because users prefer to see things in a familiar context rather than having to be trained in a new user interface every time a new system is rolled out.

A   Setting Up a UWL Development Environment

Not everyone has access to a development environment to try things out; in fact, such things may be frowned upon if you are at a customer site and involved in the support of an existing system. This appendix shows you how to download, install, and configure your own SAP NetWeaver ABAP and Java stacks so that you can create your own development environment and experiment with all of the techniques described in this book.

The development environment described here is based on the SAP NetWeaver 7.0 Trial Version editions of the ABAP and Java application servers, available from the SAP Community Network at *http://sdn.sap.com*. The ABAP server provides the SAP Business Workflow engine and comes with the SAP GUI Windows desktop client and an embedded version of the browser-based SAP GUI for HTML. The Java server provides the SAP NetWeaver Portal (including UWL), the Web Dynpro runtime, and the GPs runtime.

In terms of the hardware required to run these servers, unless you have a powerful machine with 3GB or more memory, it is not recommended to run both servers on the same machine. The ABAP server requires a machine with at least 1GB memory, and the Java server really needs 2GB to run UWL with GPs effectively.

A.1   SAP NetWeaver 7.0 ABAP Trial Version

This section shows you how to install and configure the ABAP stack so that you end up with a working development client and an activated SAP Business Workflow system.

Download and Install Software

The first thing you need to do is to go to *http://sdn.sap.com* to download and install the SAP NetWeaver ABAP stack as follows:

1. Go to the **Downloads** section (use the link on the main menu).
2. In the Download Catalog, click on the link **SAP NetWeaver Main Releases** in the **Evaluation Software** section.
3. Click on the link **SAP NetWeaver 7.0 – ABAP Trial Version**.
4. Click on the link **Click here for download**.
5. Download each of the files from the download page by selecting the relevant radio button and then clicking the **Download** button (see Figure A.1).

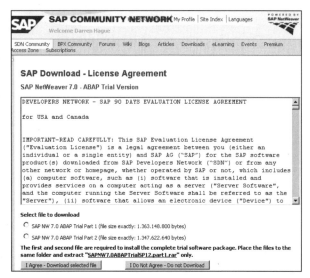

Figure A.1   Download Page for ABAP Trial Version

6. Unpack the first of the two files; the second file will be unpacked automatically.

Software to Unpack RAR Files

You may need to download additional software to unpack the two RAR files. The 7Zip software (*http://www.7-zip.org*) is a good freely available choice for this.

7. Following the instructions in the README file, install the ABAP Trial Version to c:\usr\sap (*not* the default location of C:\SAP).

8. Install SAP GUI for Windows from the Trial Version files.

9. Create a SAP Logon entry for the instance NSP you have just installed.

Set Up System Profiles

Now for a bit of Basis work — you need to set up and import the profiles containing the instance parameters that determine the low-level system behavior. There are three profiles to set up, and you need to follow the next set of steps three times, once for each profile. The three profiles are listed here:

▸ DEFAULT.PFL (Default profile)

▸ NSP_DVEBMGS02_hostname (Instance profile)

▸ START_DVEBMGS02_hostname (Startup profile)

1. Launch SAP GUI for Windows, and log in to client 000 as **SAP*** with password **minisap**.

2. Go to **Extras • Settings • Display technical names** to see the transaction codes on menus. Run transaction RZ10.

3. In Windows, look for the profile file in the folder *C:\usr\sap\NSP\SYS\profile*.

4. Enter the **Profile** name, and click **Import** (see Figure A.2).

5. At the **First maintain management data** pop-up, click **Continue**.

6. In the next window, add a description matching the profile type, select the **Profile type,** and click the **Copy** button (see Figure A.3).

7. Click the **Import** button (see Figure A.4) to specify the file from which the initial set of parameter values will be loaded.

Figure A.2   Edit Profiles

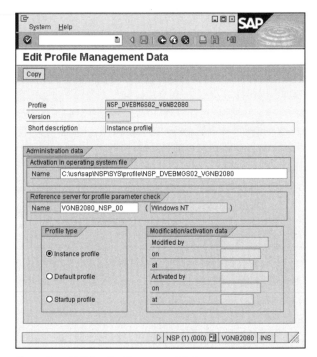

Figure A.3   Edit Profile Management Data

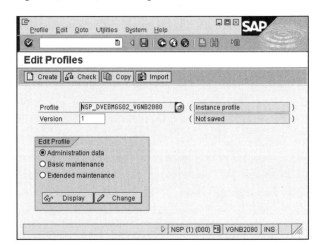

Figure A.4   Edit Profiles

8. Find the relevant profile file. In our example, it is *C:\usr\sap\NSP\SYS\profile\NSP_DVEBMGS02_VGNB2080*. Click **Copy**.

9. At the following prompt to display incorrect parameter values, click **No** (of course, in a production setting, your Basis administrator would pay more attention to this message!). The following "Profile imported" message shows you were successful, so click **Continue**.

10. In the next screen, **Edit Profiles**, click **Save**. Once again, there is no need to display incorrect parameter values, so click **No** in the following pop-up.

11. When the system asks you to activate the profile (see Figure A.5), click **Yes**.

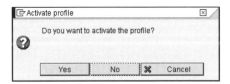

Figure A.5   Active Profile

After you have imported and activated all three profiles, you need to add a new parameter to the instance profile as follows:

1. Select the instance profile, `NSP_DVEBMGS00_hostname`.

2. Check the **Extended maintenance** radio button, followed by the **Change** button.

3. Press `F5` to create a new parameter, and set the parameter name to `login/no_automatic_user_sap-star` with value 0.

4. Click the **Copy** button, followed by clicking the **Back** button twice.

5. Click **Yes** when asked to save changes to the profile, then click **Save,** and click **Yes** to activate the resulting new profile.

6. Log out of SAPGUI.

7. If they do not already exist, create the Windows shares `sapmnt` and `saploc` at *C:\usr\sap*, giving **Full Control** permission to the **Administrators** group.

8. **Restart** the NSP instance from the SAP Management Console (see Figure A.6).

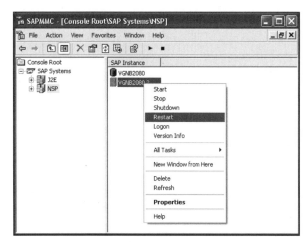

Figure A.6   Restart the NSP Instance

Apply For and Install License Key

To run the ABAP instance for more than a few days, you will need a license key from SAP. Each license key will allow the evaluation software to run for 90 more days, and you can apply for a new one each time the old one runs out.

1. Launch SAP GUI for Windows, and log in to client 000 as **SAP*** with password **minisap**.

2. Run transaction SLICENSE.

3. Follow the instructions on the screen (see Figure A.7) to request a license key.

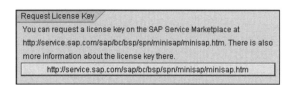

Figure A.7   Request a License Key for a Trial Version

4. Wait for an email containing the license key, and then save the license key file to disk.

5. Click the button (**Install New License**), and select the license key file.

Client Copy

Now that you have a licensed and functioning basic system, you need to copy the default client 000 to create a development client 100.

1. Launch SAP GUI for Windows, and log in to client 000 as **SAP*** with password **minisap**.

2. Run transaction SCC4, **Clients Overview**, and enter Change mode (Ctrl + F1). Click the **New Entry** button.

3. Set the client to 100 with description "UWL development" and the **Client role** set to **Customizing**. Leave the other fields as default or blank, and click **Save**.

4. Start SAP GUI, and log in to NSP, this time to the new client 100 as **SAP*** with the password **pass** (*not* minisap).

5. Run transaction SCCL, the **Local Client Copy**. Choose profile SAP_CUST, set the source client to 000, and click the **Start Immediately** button.

6. When the **Verification** prompt appears, click **Continue** (see Figure A.8).

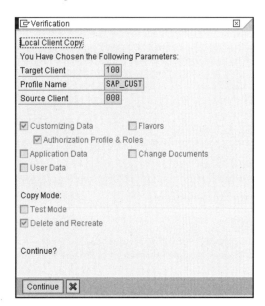

Figure A.8   Verification

7. The client copy will take several minutes, perhaps as much as an hour, depending on the power of your machine.

User Administration

Now that you've created a client in which to do your development, you'll need to set up an admin user to work with.

1. Run transaction SUGR, and create a group SUPER.

2. Run transaction SU01, and create a user for yourself; assigning profiles SAP_ALL and SAP_NEW, in group SUPER, will give you all the admin rights you could need.

3. You will first be prompted to create a Company (see Figure A.9 and Figure A.10), in the pop-up, so enter a sample company name.

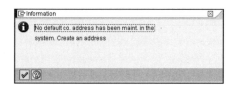

Figure A.9   Create a User

Figure A.10   Company Name

4. After you have entered a company name, the only mandatory fields are the **Country** and **Time zone** (see Figure A.11).

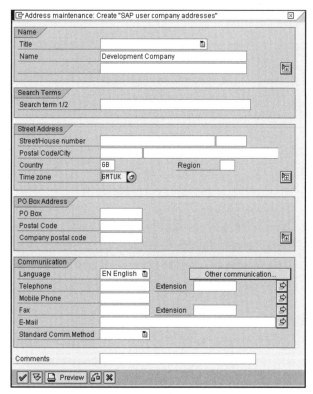

Figure A.11   Address Maintenance

5. Log in to the new client as the newly created admin user. Being the first login of the user, you will be prompted to change the password.

Setting Up SAP Business Workflow on the New Client
Now that you have a client for doing development and an admin user set up, it's time to get the SAP Business Workflow engine working.

1. Run transaction SWU3, the **Automatic Workflow Customizing**, and execute auto-customizing by pressing F9. The node **Maintain Runtime Environment** should now be green (see Figure A.12).

Figure A.12   Transaction SWU3 After Initial Auto-Customizing

2. Expand the node **Maintain Definition Environment**, select **Maintain prefix numbers**, and then execute the activity (F8).

3. Click the button (**Display Change**) to enter **Change** mode, and then click the button (**Create**), as shown in Figure A.13.

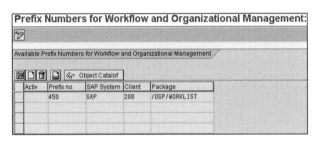

Figure A.13   Setting Up Prefix Numbers

4. Enter Prefix number "900" for NSP Client 100, and then click the **Save** button. In the subsequent pop-up, click the **Local Object** button, and in the next pop-up click the **Continue** button.

5. Click the **Back** button to go back to the **Automatic Workflow Customizing** main screen.

6. Run transaction SE38. Enter program name RHSOBJCH, and click **Execute**. When the program runs, click the button **Select All**, followed by **Adjust**.

7. Run transaction SWU3 once again, and this time, under the **Maintain Definition Environment** node, execute the activity **Check entries from HR Control tables**. Select the node **Maintain Additional Settings and Services**, and press F9 (**Auto-customizing**).

8. Execute the activity **Maintain Web Server**, and then click the **New Entries** button.

9. Set the **Service** to **Webflow (Intranet)**, and the web server address to *http://<hostname>:80xx/* where xx is the instance number, for example, *http://workflow.fortybeans.com:8000/*. Leave the other entries as their default values (see Figure A.14).

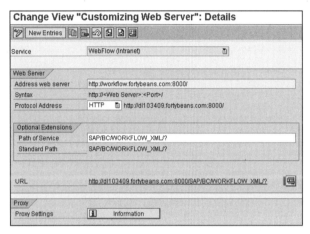

Figure A.14   Maintaining Web Server Settings

10. Click **Save**, and at the **Prompt for Customizing Request** pop-up, click the **Own Requests** button. You may need to create a dummy transport request at this point (click the **Create** button, and enter some random description), which you can then select.

11. Click **Back** until you are back at the **Automatic Workflow Customizing** screen. Execute the activity **Maintain standard domain for internet mails**, and enter a default domain, such as fortybeans.com.

12. Now select the node **Classify Tasks as General**, and press F9 for auto-customizing.

13. Select the node **Guided procedures**, and press F9 for auto-customizing; this leaves only **Maintain Guided Procedures gateway** as a red cross, which can be left as-is for the time being.

Check the Workflow Setup
The last part of setting up the workflow system is to make sure that everything works okay, and there is a very simple example workflow you can run to check this.

1. In transaction SWU3, click the icon (**Start verification workflow**).

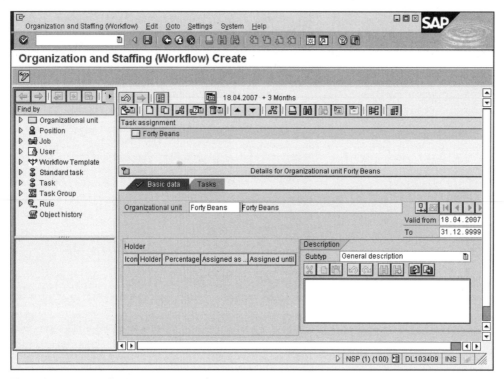

Figure A.15   Naming the Root Organizational Unit

2. When asked, click **Yes** to **Activate event linkage for this workflow**. Wait for a few minutes for the workflow engine to initialize.

3. Click the 🗒 icon (**SAP Business Workplace**) to go to the SAP Inbox, where you should see an item labeled "First step in workflow verification."

A.2   Setting Up an Organizational Plan for the Notification of Absence Example

In this section, we'll create a small organization with one chief, Ebenezer Scrooge, and a clerk, Bob Cratchit, who reports to the chief. For more details on this procedure, see the section **Business Task Management • Reference • Tutorials • Business Workflow – Tutorials • Tutorial: Maintaining the Organizational Plan • Unit 1: Creating an Organizational Plan** in the SAP Help Portal.

1. Run transaction SU01, and create the users Ebenezer Scrooge with user ID ESCROOGE1, and Bob Cratchit with user ID BCRATCHIT2. We are not too concerned with authorizations in this book, so let's keep things simple: in the **Profiles** tab and just assign the profiles SAP_ALL and SAP_NEW to each user.

2. Run transaction PPOC to create an organizational plan, and accept the default validity dates (today until 31.12.9999).

3. Fill in the details for the root object **New org unit,** which is created by default (see Figure A.15), and click **Save**.

4. From the **Edit** menu, select **Create jobs**.

5. Create the jobs **Manager** and **Clerk**, as shown in Figure A.16.

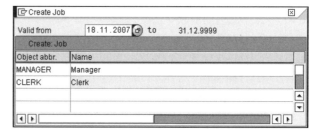

Figure A.16   Create the Jobs Manager and Clerk

6. Back at the PPOC main screen, click the 🗒 button (**Goto**), and select the option **Staff assignments (list)**.

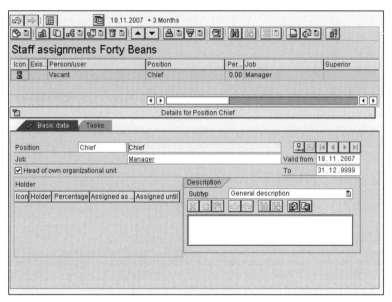

Figure A.17   Creating the Chief Position

7. Click the ⬚ button (**Create Position**), create a position **Chief** with job **Manager**, and select the checkbox **Head of own organizational unit** (see Figure A.17).

8. Click the ⬚ button (**Assign**). In the resulting dialog box, find the user ESCROOGE1, and assign that user to the position. Click **Save**.

9. Repeat the previous two steps to create the position **Assistant** with job **Clerk** (but don't check the box for **Head of own organizational unit** this time), and assign the user BCRATCHIT2.

10. The staff assignments should now look like Figure A.18.

Staff assignments Forty Beans

Icon	Exis...	Person/user	Position	Percentage	Job	Superior
🔲		Ebenezer Scrooge	Chief	100.00	Manager	
🔲		Bob Cratchit	Assistant	100.00	Clerk	Ebenezer Scrooge

Figure A.18   Staff Assignments for the Forty Beans Organization

A.3   Configure the SAP Notification of Absence Workflow

Now that you have set up the organizational structure, the next step is to configure the demonstration workflow, processing a notification of absence, which is used as the main example in this book. This configuration is based on the documentation in the SAP Help Portal at **Embedded Processes (SAP Business Workflow) • Reference • SAP Business Workflow Examples • Demo Example: Processing a Notification of Absence • Preparation and Customizing.**

1. Run transaction SPRO, and click the button to select the **SAP Reference IMG.**

2. Navigate to the task **SAP NetWeaver • Application Server • Business Management • SAP Business Workflow • Perform task-specific Customizing,** and execute it (alternatively, just run transaction OOCU).

3. Navigate to the SAP component BC-BMT-WFM (**Basis Components • Business Management • SAP Business Workflow**), and click **Assign Agents** for that component (see Figure A.19).

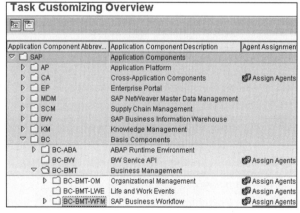

Figure A.19   Assign Agents for BC-CMT-WFM

4. Select task **TS30000016,** and click the ![icon] icon (**Create agent assignment**). Select the object type **Job,** and then assign the job of **Manager** that you created in the previous section.

5. Select task TS30000017, and click the **Attributes** button. Select the radio button **General Task,** and then click the **Transfer** button.

6. Run transaction SWDD, and enter the workflow code WS30000015, followed by clicking the ![icon] icon (**Basic data**).

7. Go to the **Start Events** tab, and click the ◇ icon (**Activate**) on the **FORMABSENC** row (see Figure A.20) to change the event status from Inactive to Active. You will need to assign a dummy transport request when prompted.

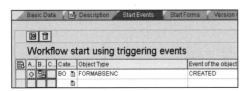

Figure A.20   Activating the Start Event for the Workflow

8. Go back to the **Workflow Builder** screen, click the ![icon] icon (**Generate and activate runtime version**), and then exit the transaction.

9. Test the workflow by logging on as BCRATCHIT2 and running transaction SWXF to create an absence. When this has been created and saved, log in as ESCROOGE1, and run SBWP to check that the approval task appears in the SAP Inbox.

A.4   SAP NetWeaver 7.0 Java Trial Version

This section shows you how to install and configure the Java stack so that you end up with a working portal with UWL, Web Dynpro, and GP functionality.

Download and Install Software

The first thing you need to do is to go to *http://sdn.sap.com* to download and install the SAP NetWeaver Java stack as follows.

1. Go to the **Downloads** section (use the link on the main menu). In the Download Catalog, click on the link **SAP**

NetWeaver Main Releases in the Evaluation Software section.

2. Click on the link **SAP NetWeaver 7.0 – Java Trial Version** (make sure you get the 7.0 version, not the 2004 version).

3. Click on the link **Click here for download,** and download each of the files from the download page by selecting the relevant radio button (see Figure A.21).

Figure A.21   Download Page for Java Trial Version

4. Unpack the first of the two Java edition files; the second file will be unpacked automatically.

5. Following the instructions in the README file, install the Java Trial Version to C:\usr\sap.

6. Unpack and install the Developer Studio if you want to develop Web Dynpro applications, portal applications, or UWL connectors.

Tip

You may get better performance by installing the SAP NetWeaver Developer Studio on a different machine from the SAP NetWeaver Application Server Java.

Set Up Single Sign-on

The final stage of setting up your development environment is to establish a single sign-on connection between the Java and ABAP servers. For single sign-on to work, you need to make sure the users are set up correctly. See the next box "User Management" for details.

User Management

For single sign-on to work properly, you must ensure that each user is created on both the ABAP and Java servers with the same user ID. One way of achieving this is to configure the Java UME to use an ABAP data source, which is beyond the scope of this book.

The alternative is to manually create users in each system with the same details; in this case, that means creating users ESCROOGE1 and BCRATCHIT2 in the portal to match the users you created earlier when configuring the SAP Business Workflow (see Section A.2).

1. In the ABAP instance, run transaction RZ10 in the SAP GUI, and select the **Instance profile**. Choose **Extended maintenance,** and click the **Change** button (see Figure A.22).

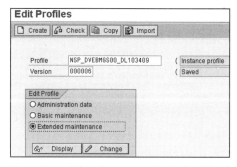

Figure A.22   Select the Instance Profile for Extended Maintenance

2. Make sure the profile parameters shown in Table A.1 are set.

Parameter Name	Parameter Value
login/create_sso2_ticket	2
login/accept_sso2_ticket	1

Table A.1   Profile Parameters for Single Sign-On

3. Save and activate the new profile, and restart the ABAP instance.
4. Log in to the SAP NetWeaver Java portal instance as an administrator, and navigate to **System Administration** • **System Configuration** • **Keystore Administration**.
5. Click the button **Download verify.der File** and save the resulting ZIP file to disk (see Figure A.23).
6. Extract the file verify.der from the downloaded file.

7. In the ABAP instance, run transaction STRUSTSSO2 in the SAP GUI, and choose **Certificate** • **Import** from the menu.

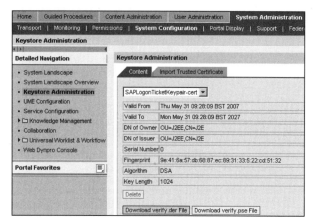

Figure A.23   Downloading the Portal Certificate

8. Select the file verify.der, making sure the file format is set to **Binary**, and press the ⏎ key to import the certificate.
9. Click the button **Add to Certificate List**, and you should see the line OU=J2EE, CN=J2E appear in the certificate list.
10. Click the button **Add to ACL**, and in the resulting dialog box, set the System ID to **J2E** and the client to **000** (see Figure A.24).

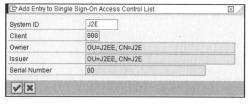

Figure A.24   Adding the Certificate to the Access Control List

11. Click **Save,** and then exit the transaction.

That's all there is to it. You should now have SAP NetWeaver Java and ABAP instances with the SAP NetWeaver Portal and SAP Business Workflow set up, and you're ready to start exploring the examples used in this book.

B References and Further Reading

This appendix gives details of various online resources and reference information to help you find out more about the Universal Worklist (UWL). Section B.1 contains web links for all of the SAP documentation mentioned in the rest of the book; Section B.2 gives some additional links to useful areas on the SAP Community Network; Section B.3 lists some particularly relevant SAP notes; and Section B.4 gives an exhaustive list of the SAP_WAPI and UWL function modules in SAP Business Workflow.

Because web links can change over time, the best place to go for an up-to-date list is the website for this book. The website will also be much more convenient because you can just click on the links there instead of having to type them in.

B.1 SAP Documentation

Throughout the book, you will have noticed many references to documentation in the SAP Help Portal or the SAP Community Network. This section, including Table B.1 to Table B.5, contains tables of all of those references to save you the effort of searching for them.

Documentation Title	Link
Business Task Management • Universal Worklist Configuration • Advanced Configuration • Removing Actions from the UWL Display	http://help.sap.com/saphelp_nw2004s/helpdata/en/09/6d6b17b29b4eef83a553acaa52f668/frameset.htm
Business Task Management • Universal Worklist Configuration • Advanced Configuration • Task Launch Customization • Action Handlers	http://help.sap.com/saphelp_nw04s/helpdata/en/2c/05b15de3864040a9426788a12699b3/frameset.htm
Business Task Management • Universal Worklist Configuration • Configuration DTD	http://help.sap.com/saphelp_nw2004s/helpdata/en/d2/69c045994448adad27d36c4154fe74/frameset.htm
ITS Administrator's Guide • Internet Transaction Server (ITS) • Internet Application Component (IAC)	http://help.sap.com/saphelp_nw04/helpdata/en/44/216fe21784648ee10000000a1553f7/frameset.htm
Portal Development Manual • Core Development Tasks • Connecting to Backend Systems • Application Integrator • Component com.sap.portal.appintegrator.sap.Generic	http://help.sap.com/saphelp_nw04s/helpdata/en/36/5e3842134bad04e10000000a1550b0/frameset.htm
SAProuter • Using SAProuter • Route Strings	http://help.sap.com/saphelp_nw2004s/helpdata/en/4f/992de4446d11d189700000e8322d00/frameset.htm
iViews • Creating iViews • Creating Web-based URL iViews	http://help.sap.com/saphelp_nw2004s/helpdata/en/f5/eb51730e6a11d7b84900047582c9f7/frameset.htm
SAP Business Workflow • Reference Documentation • Workflow Builder • Using Web Services	http://help.sap.com/saphelp_nw04/helpdata/en/68/d4623c046a9b67e10000000a11402f/frameset.htm
Alert Management (BC-SRV-GBT-ALM)	http://help.sap.com/saphelp_nw04/helpdata/en/3f/81023cfa699508e10000000a11402f/frameset.htm

Table B.1 SAP Documentation Referred to in Chapter 2

Documentation Title	Link
Embedded Processes (SAP Business Workflow) • Reference • SAP Business Workflow Examples • Demo Example: Processing a Notification of Absence • Preparation and Customizing	http://help.sap.com/saphelp_nw2004s/helpdata/en/04/928dfa46f311d189470000e829fbbd/frameset.htm
Business Task Management • Reference • Tutorials • Business Workflow – Tutorials • Tutorial: Workflow Modeling	http://help.sap.com/saphelp_nw04s/helpdata/en/fb/135983457311d189440000e829fbbd/frameset.htm
Java Development Manual • Reference • Appendix • UME Reference • Logical Attributes	http://help.sap.com/saphelp_nw2004s/helpdata/en/e6/d75d3760735b41be930f2dddae3126/frameset.htm
UWL API Documentation for Action Handlers	http://help.sap.com/javadocs/NW04S/current/uw/com/sap/netweaver/bc/uwl/config/doc-files/ActionHandlers.html
Business Task Management • Universal Worklist Configuration • Advanced Configuration • Task Launch Configuration • Standard Item Attributes	http://help.sap.com/saphelp_nw2004s/helpdata/en/b0/9cb51c06784c06a2066d7eb9e537e1/frameset.htm

Table B.2 SAP Documentation Referred to in Chapter 3

Documentation Title	Link
Developing Third-Party Connectors for the Universal Worklist – Webinar Details	https://www.sdn.sap.com/irj/sdn/go/portal/prtroot/docs/library/uuid/e0f68fa9-f962-2910-1084-f53ae40685a7
Connecting SAP Office Mail to the Universal Worklist	http://help.sap.com/javadocs/NW04S/SPS09/uw/UWL_API_SAPOfficeMailExample.pdf (https://www.sdn.sap.com/irj/sdn/download-item?rid=/webcontent/uuid/e3ca8bd2-0d01-0010-b885-943341cd4b9c for the SAP Office connector component itself)
Universal Worklist API	http://help.sap.com/javadocs/NW04S/SPS09/uw/index.html
SDN BPEL4People Page	https://www.sdn.sap.com/irj/sdn/bpel4people
Usage Guide for Guided Procedures on SAP NetWeaver 7.0	https://www.sdn.sap.com/irj/sdn/go/portal/prtroot/docs/library/uuid/e080a639-6e21-2a10-91b7-d0b72b32303d
CAF Knowledge Center	https://www.sdn.sap.com/irj/sdn/platform?rid=/webcontent/uuid/be8a25c6-0601-0010-a49c-afd1f2500f84
Developing, Configuring, and Adapting Applications • Creating Composite Applications • CAF-GP: Configuration Guide • Parameter Configuration • Configuring Guided Procedures with the Universal Worklist	http://help.sap.com/saphelp_nw04s/helpdata/en/43/ef06a7860c7061e10000000a1553f6/frameset.htm
Power User's Guide • Developing, Configuring and Adapting Applications • Process Modeling	http://help.sap.com/saphelp_nw04s/helpdata/en/1b/d78041a17e060de10000000a1550b0/frameset.htm
Creating Callable Objects in the GP Design Time	http://help.sap.com/saphelp_nw04s/helpdata/en/da/a680415dc6050de10000000a1550b0/frameset.htm
Creating Composite Applications • Developing Composite Applications with CAF GP • Reference • Tutorials • Developing Your First Process • Setting Up Mail Templates • Replacements	http://help.sap.com/saphelp_nw2004s/helpdata/en/5d/a71342cb385333e10000000a155106/frameset.htm

Table B.3 SAP Documentation Referred to in Chapter 4

Documentation Title	Link
Business Task Management • Universal Worklist Configuration • Optional Configuration • Enabling Delta Pull Mechanism	http://help.sap.com/saphelp_nw04s/helpdata/en/eb/101fa0a53244deb955f6f91929e400/frameset.htm

Table B.4 SAP Documentation Referred to in Chapter 5

Documentation Title	Link
SAPconnect (BC-SRV-COM) • Administration • Settings for Sending Using the SMTP Plug-In	http://help.sap.com/saphelp_nw2004s/helpdata/en/c7/ 92e93ac678601be10000000a11402f/frameset.htm
Extended Notifications for SAP Business Workflow • Integration • Enabling Communication • Extended Notifications for SAP Business Workflow	http://help.sap.com/saphelp_nw70/helpdata/en/d5/ 581ee8d56f1247bf34cfcd66d16d81/frameset.htm
Example: Notifications for Leave Requests	http://help.sap.com/saphelp_nw70/helpdata/en/0f/ dd9f40eb72371be10000000a1550b0/frameset.htm
SAP NetWeaver Composition Environment Library • Administrator's Guide • Configuration for CE Additional Components • Configuring Voice-Enabled Applications • Configuring SAP NetWeaver AS	http://help.sap.com/saphelp_nwce10/helpdata/en/45/ aafabab8f52e78e10000000a155369/frameset.htm
SAP NetWeaver Composition Environment Library • Developer's Guide • Developing and Composing Applications • Developing Voice-Enabled Applications	http://help.sap.com/saphelp_nwce10/helpdata/en/45/ 65aa219ead2f95e10000000a155369/frameset.htm
SAP NetWeaver Voice White Paper at SDN	https://www.sdn.sap.com/irj/servlet/prt/portal/prtroot/docs/library/ uuid/eac9cf35-0801-0010-918b-ab231eba0bd0

Table B.5 SAP Documentation Referred to in Chapter 6

B.2 SAP Community Network Content

Questions and answers on the UWL appear in the following forums on the SAP Developer Network (http:// sdn.sap.com):

▸ **Expert Forums • Portal • Portal Implementation**
▸ **Expert Forums • Portal • Knowledge Management & Collaboration**
▸ **Expert Forums • Portal • Portal Content Development**
▸ **Expert Forums • SAP NetWeaver • BPM and Workflow**
▸ **Expert Forums • SAP NetWeaver • Composite Application Framework**

There are a few eLearning resources available (see Table B.6).

The Universal Worklist Wiki on SDN is at https:// www.sdn.sap.com/irj/sdn/wiki?path=/display/BPX/ BPX%2bUWL.

B.3 Useful SAP Notes

Here is a list of some of the most useful SAP notes relating to the UWL (see Table B.7). It's worth checking these regularly, or at least whenever you have a problem, to see if they have been updated.

Documentation Title	Link
Troubleshooting EP Top Incidents – Webinar Replay	https://www.sdn.sap.com/irj/sdn/go/portal/prtroot/docs/library/ uuid/5854a490-0201-0010-5da9-cb399f9b67a8
Developing Third-Party Connectors for the Universal Worklist – Webinar Replay	https://www.sdn.sap.com/irj/sdn/go/portal/prtroot/docs/library/ uuid/d0fe7ef7-b37d-2910-239c-a325b61ccea4
Create Master Data Centrally Using Guided Procedures Config UWL Connector	https://www.sdn.sap.com/irj/sdn/go/portal/prtroot/docs/library/ uuid/892b1b79-0d01-0010-37a9-e546b8fc2a5f

Table B.6 SDN eLearning Resources

SAP Note	Title
SAP Note 300645	Up/Download Functions in ITS Context
SAP Note 314568	SAP GUI for HTML Functionality/Limitations /Sp. Behavior
SAP Note 454939	SAP GUI for Java Limitations
SAP Note 794439	Universal Worklist Support for SAP Business Workflow
SAP Note 812079	EP 6.0: Central Note for Ad hoc Workflow (Java Workflow)
SAP Note 883558	Maintaining Substitutes in the Universal Worklist
SAP Note 888457	NW2004s: Universal Worklist Release Note
SAP Note 921758	How to Access the Universal Worklist Integration API
SAP Note 921870	The API to the Universal Worklist
SAP Note 941589	UWL: Administrative and End User Roles
SAP Note 942571	UWL Service User Maintenance with CUA
SAP Note 945484	How to Receive Office Notifications in a Universal Worklist

Table B.7   Useful SAP Notes

B.4   SAP Business Workflow and UWL Function Modules

Table B.8 lists all of the function modules with UWL or SAP_WAPI in the name. Glancing down this table can save you having to go into transaction SE37 and hitting F4 to search.

Function Module Name	Short Text for Function Module
Function group SWF_PLOG_API	
SWF_PLOG_GET_LOG_UWL	
Function group SWN_UWL_ADHOC	
SWN_UWL_REGISTER_COMPLETED	
SWN_UWL_REGISTER_STARTED	
Function group SWN_UWL_URL_GEN	
SWN_UWL_SERVER_TYPE_DATA_GET	
Function group SWN_UWL_WL	
SWN_UWL_GET_OUTBOX	
SWN_UWL_GET_RESUBMISSIONS	
SWN_UWL_GET_WORKLIST	
Function group SWRC	Workflow Interfaces: Work List Client
SAP_WAPI_ATTACHMENT_ADD	

Table B.8   UWL and Workflow Function Modules

Function Module Name	Short Text for Function Module
SAP_WAPI_ATTACHMENT_ADD_REF	
SAP_WAPI_ATTACHMENT_DELETE	
SAP_WAPI_CHANGE_WORKITEM_PRIO	Workflow Interfaces: Change Priority of Work Item
SAP_WAPI_COUNT_WORKITEMS	Workflow Interfaces: Number of Work Items for User
SAP_WAPI_END_RESUBMISSION	
SAP_WAPI_EXECUTE_WORKITEM	Workflow Interfaces: Execute Work Item
SAP_WAPI_FORWARD_WORKITEM	Workflow Interfaces: Forward Work Item
SAP_WAPI_GET_ATTACHMENTS	Workflow Interfaces: Read Attachment for Work Item
SAP_WAPI_GET_DEADLINES	Workflow Interfaces: Read Work Item Deadlines
SAP_WAPI_GET_HEADER	Workflow Interfaces: Read Work Item Header
SAP_WAPI_GET_METHODS	Workflow Interfaces: Read Work Item Methods
SAP_WAPI_GET_MULTI_EXEC_GUID	
SAP_WAPI_GET_OBJECTS	Workflow Interfaces: Read Work Item Objects
SAP_WAPI_GET_WORKITEM_DETAIL	
SAP_WAPI_PUT_BACK_WORKITEM	Workflow Interfaces: Replace Work Item
SAP_WAPI_REJECT_WORKITEM	Workflow Interfaces: Reserve Work Item
SAP_WAPI_RESERVE_WORKITEM	Workflow Interfaces: Reserve Work Item
SAP_WAPI_RESUBMIT_WORKITEM	
SAP_WAPI_SET_WORKITEM_COMPLETD	Workflow Interfaces: Set Work Item to Completed
SAP_WAPI_SET_WORKITEM_STATUS	
SAP_WAPI_WORKITEM_DESCRIPTION	Workflow Interfaces: Read Work Item Description
SAP_WAPI_WORKITEM_RECIPIENTS	Workflow Interfaces: Read Work Item Recipients
Function group SWRI	
SAP_WAPI_GET_DEPENDENT_WIS	
SAP_WAPI_OBJECTS_IN_WORKITEM	
SAP_WAPI_WORKITEMS_BY_DEADLINE	
SAP_WAPI_WORKITEMS_BY_ERROR	
SAP_WAPI_WORKITEMS_BY_FREQUENC	
SAP_WAPI_WORKITEMS_BY_TASK	
SAP_WAPI_WORKITEMS_TO_OBJECT	
Function group SWRR	Workflow Interfaces: Runtime
SAP_WAPI_ASYNC_RULE_COMPLETE	
SAP_WAPI_CREATE_EVENT	Workflow Interfaces: Create Event

Table B.8   UWL and Workflow Function Modules (cont.)

Function Module Name	Short Text for Function Module
SAP_WAPI_DECISION_COMPLETE	
SAP_WAPI_DECISION_READ	
SAP_WAPI_GET_EXCLUDED_FUNCTION	
SAP_WAPI_GET_PROPERTY	
SAP_WAPI_GET_TASK_CNT_SCHEMA	
SAP_WAPI_GET_WI_CNT_SCHEMA	
SAP_WAPI_READ_CONTAINER	Workflow Interfaces: Read Container
SAP_WAPI_SET_ERROR	
SAP_WAPI_SET_MESSAGE	
SAP_WAPI_START_WORKFLOW	Workflow Interfaces: Start Workflow
SAP_WAPI_WORKITEM_COMPLETE	
SAP_WAPI_WORKITEM_CONFIRM	
SAP_WAPI_WORKITEM_DELETE	
SAP_WAPI_WRITE_CONTAINER	Workflow Interfaces: Write Container
Function group SWRS	
SAP_WAPI_SUBSTITUTES_GET	
SAP_WAPI_SUBSTITUTE_ACTIVATE	
SAP_WAPI_SUBSTITUTE_DEACTIVATE	
SAP_WAPI_SUBSTITUTE_DELETE	
SAP_WAPI_SUBSTITUTE_MAINTAIN	
SAP_WAPI_SUBSTITUTE_PROF_GET	
SAP_WAPI_SUBSTITUTIONS_GET	
SAP_WAPI_SUBSTITUTION_ADOPT	
SAP_WAPI_SUBSTITUTION_END	
Function group SWRW	Workflow Interfaces: Worklist
SAP_WAPI_CREATE_OUTBOX	
SAP_WAPI_CREATE_WORKLIST	Workflow Interfaces: Set Up Worklist for User
SAP_WAPI_FORWARDING_INFO_GET	
SAP_WAPI_GET_RESUBMISSIONS	
SAP_WAPI_GET_WI_AGENTS	
SAP_WAPI_GET_WI_ALL	
SAP_WAPI_GET_WI_DELTA	
SAP_WAPI_GET_WI_XML	

Table B.8 UWL and Workflow Function Modules (cont.)

Function Module Name	Short Text for Function Module
Function group SWR_WS	
SAP_WAPI_LAUNCH_URL_GET	
Function group UWLCONN	Enhanced Connection for UWL
UWL_ASSIGN_USERS_CHANNEL	Adding User to a UWL Channel
UWL_ASSIGN_USER_CHANNEL	Adding User to a UWL Channel
UWL_CREATE_SERVICE_USER	Creating UWL Service User
UWL_DEL_ALL_USERS_FROM_CHANNEL	Remove All Users from UWL Channel
UWL_DEL_USER_FROM_CHANNEL	Remove User from UWL Channel
UWL_DETECT_BWF_DELTA_JOB	Check Whether the Required BWF Delta Job Is Scheduled
UWL_GET_ITEMS_PROXY	Prototype for UWL Proxy
UWL_GET_USERS_IN_CHANNEL	Prototype for Tracking User in Channel
UWL_UPDATE_USER_TIME	Update User Access Time with UWL
Function group UWLPERF	Bundling of FM for Performance Reason
UWL_DOCUMENTS_HEADER_READ	Read headers of Multiple Attachments
UWL_SWO_INVOKE	Wrap Around Bundling for SWO_INVOKE
Function group UWLTASK	ABAP Enabling of Ad Hoc Workflow
CPE_UWLTASK_CREATE	ABAP Enabling of Ad Hoc Workflow
CPE_UWLTASK_CREATE_LOGENTRY	Create Log Entry for Creation of a CPE Task for Display in UWL

Table B.8   UWL and Workflow Function Modules (cont.)

C   Source Code for Web Dynpro Action Handler

This appendix lists in full the four Java Web Dynpro helper methods from Chapter 3. Only the comments were included in Chapter 3 for space reasons.

```
private void getWorkitemDetail(String workitem_id)
{
  // Call SAP_WAPI_GET_WORKITEM_DETAIL with workitem_id as input
  Sap_Wapi_Get_Workitem_Detail_Input wiDetailInput =
    new Sap_Wapi_Get_Workitem_Detail_Input();
  wdContext.nodeSap_Wapi_Get_Workitem_Detail_Input().bind(wiDetailInput);
  wiDetailInput.setWorkitem_Id(workitem_id);
  try {
    wdContext.currentSap_Wapi_Get_Workitem_Detail_InputElement().modelObject().execute();
  } catch (WDDynamicRFCExecuteException e) {
    String errorMessage = "ERROR calling SAP_WAPI_GET_WORKITEM_DETAIL: "+e.getMessage();
    logger.errorT(errorMessage);
    e.printStackTrace();
    manager.raiseException(errorMessage, true);
  }
  wdContext.nodeDetailOutput().invalidate();

  // Retrieve note_count and wi_stat from the RFC call output
  numAttachments = wdContext.currentWorkitem_DetailElement().getNote_Count();
  workitemStatus = wdContext.currentWorkitem_DetailElement().getWi_Stat();
}
```

Listing C.1   getWorkitemDetail()

```
private String getFormId(String workitem_id)
{
  // Call SAP_WAPI_GET_OBJECTS with workitem_id as input
  Sap_Wapi_Get_Objects_Input wiObjectsInput = new Sap_Wapi_Get_Objects_Input();
  wdContext.nodeSap_Wapi_Get_Objects_Input().bind(wiObjectsInput);
  wiObjectsInput.setWorkitem_Id(workitem_id);
  try {
    wdContext.currentSap_Wapi_Get_Objects_InputElement().modelObject().execute();
  } catch (WDDynamicRFCExecuteException e) {
    String errorMessage = "ERROR calling SAP_WAPI_GET_OBJECTS: "+e.getMessage();
    logger.errorT(errorMessage);
    e.printStackTrace();
    manager.raiseException(errorMessage, true);
  }
  wdContext.nodeLeading_Object_2().invalidate();

  // Retrieve Typeid and Instid from the RFC output, as formType and formNumber
  String formType = wdContext.currentLeading_Object_2Element().getTypeid();
  String formNumber = wdContext.currentLeading_Object_2Element().getInstid();

  // If the form type is an absence form, return the form number.
  if (ABSENCE_FORM_TYPE.equals(formType))
  {
    return formNumber;
  }
  else
  {   // Otherwise, report an error.
    String errorMessage = "Error: SAP_WAPI_GET_OBJECTS has a leading object of type "
      + formType;
    logger.errorT(errorMessage);
    manager.raiseException(errorMessage, true);
    return null;
  }
}
```

Listing C.2   getFormId()

```
private String getWorkitemDescription(String workitem_id)
{
  // Call SAP_WAPI_WORKITEM_DESCRIPTION with workitem_id as input
  Sap_Wapi_Workitem_Description_Input wiDescriptionlInput =
    new Sap_Wapi_Workitem_Description_Input();
  wdContext.nodeSap_Wapi_Workitem_Description_Input().bind(wiDescriptionlInput);
  wiDescriptionlInput.setWorkitem_Id(workitem_id);
  try {
    wdContext.currentSap_Wapi_Workitem_Description_InputElement().modelObject().execute();
  } catch (WDDynamicRFCExecuteException e) {
    String errorMessage = "ERROR calling SAP_WAPI_WORKITEM_DESCRIPTION: "+e.getMessage();
    logger.errorT(errorMessage);
    e.printStackTrace();
    manager.raiseException(errorMessage, true);
  }
  wdContext.nodeDescriptionOutput().invalidate();

  String description = new String();

  // Build up a description line by line from the RFC Text_Lines table
  IText_LinesNode lines = wdContext.nodeText_Lines();
  for (int lineIdx = 0; lineIdx < lines.size(); lineIdx++)
  {
    IText_LinesElement lineElem = lines.getText_LinesElementAt(lineIdx);
    description += (lineElem.getTextline().trim())+" ";
  }


  // Return the description as a string
  return description;

}
```

Listing C.3   getWorkitemDescription()

```
private void getFormDetails(String form_id)
{
  // Call SWK_DEMO_FORMABS_READ with form_id as input
  Swk_Demo_Formabs_Read_Input formreadInput = new Swk_Demo_Formabs_Read_Input();
  wdContext.nodeSwk_Demo_Formabs_Read_Input().bind(formreadInput);
  formreadInput.setIm_Formnumber(form_id);
  try {
    wdContext.currentSwk_Demo_Formabs_Read_InputElement().modelObject().execute();
  } catch (WDDynamicRFCExecuteException e) {
    String errorMessage = "ERROR calling SWK_DEMO_FORMABS_READ: "+e.getMessage();
    logger.errorT(errorMessage);
    e.printStackTrace();
    manager.raiseException(errorMessage, true);
  }
  wdContext.nodeE_Formdata().invalidate();

  // Set the leave and visibility context attributes
  //  according to whether each start date is null or not
  Date first1 = wdContext.currentE_FormdataElement().getFirstday1();
  if (first1 != null)
  {
    // Build up description of the first leave entry from RFC output values
    //  Firstday1, Lastday1, and Abshours1
    logger.debugT("Date Firstday1 is "+first1);
    String leave1First = dateFormat.format(first1);
    String leave1Last = dateFormat.format(wdContext.currentE_FormdataElement().getLastday1());
    String leave1Hours = wdContext.currentE_FormdataElement().getAbshours1().toString();
    String leave1 = "Leave 1: from " + leave1First + " to "
      + leave1Last + " (" + leave1Hours + " hours)";

    wdContext.currentContextElement().setLeave1(leave1);
    wdContext.currentContextElement().setLeave1_visibility(WDVisibility.VISIBLE);
  }
  else
  {
    wdContext.currentContextElement().setLeave1_visibility(WDVisibility.NONE);
  }
```

Listing C.4 getFormDetails()

```
Date first2 = wdContext.currentE_FormdataElement().getFirstday2();
if (first2 != null)
{
  // Build up description of the second leave entry from RFC output values
  //  Firstday2, Lastday2, and Abshours2
  logger.debugT("Date Firstday2 is "+first1);
  String leave2First = dateFormat.format(first2);
  String leave2Last = dateFormat.format(wdContext.currentE_FormdataElement().getLastday2());
  String leave2Hours = wdContext.currentE_FormdataElement().getAbshours2().toString();
  String leave2 = "Leave 2: from " + leave2First + " to "
    + leave2Last + " (" + leave2Hours + " hours)";

  wdContext.currentContextElement().setLeave2(leave2);
  wdContext.currentContextElement().setLeave2_visibility(WDVisibility.VISIBLE);
}
else
{
  wdContext.currentContextElement().setLeave2_visibility(WDVisibility.NONE);
}


Date first3 = wdContext.currentE_FormdataElement().getFirstday3();
if (first3 != null)
{
  // Build up description of the third leave entry from RFC output values
  //  Firstday3, Lastday3, and Abshours3
  logger.debugT("Date Firstday3 is "+first1);
  String leave3First = dateFormat.format(first3);
  String leave3Last = dateFormat.format(wdContext.currentE_FormdataElement().getLastday3());
  String leave3Hours = wdContext.currentE_FormdataElement().getAbshours3().toString();
  String leave3 = "Leave 3: from " + leave3First + " to "
    + leave3Last + " ("+leave3Hours + " hours)";

  wdContext.currentContextElement().setLeave3(leave3);
  wdContext.currentContextElement().setLeave3_visibility(WDVisibility.VISIBLE);
}
else
```

Listing C.4   getFormDetails() (cont.)

```
  {
    wdContext.currentContextElement().setLeave3_visibility(WDVisibility.NONE);
  }

}
```

Listing C.4   getFormDetails() (cont.)

Index

ISBN 978-1-59229-146-5
1st edition 2008
© 2008 by Galileo Press GmbH
SAP PRESS is an imprint of Galileo Press,
Boston (MA), USA
Bonn, Germany

Editor Stefan Proksch
Technical Reviewer Jocelyn Dart, SAP
Copy Editor Julie McNamee, Hope, IN
Cover Design Vera Brauner
Production Vera Brauner
Printed in Germany